Tue Greenfort

Eine Berggeschichte

*dornbirn***kunstraum**

VERLAG *für* **MODERNE KUNST**

	Inhalt		Contents
06	Severin Dünser Eine Berggeschichte	06	Severin Dünser A Mountain Story
26	Peder Anker, Universität Oslo Wissenschaft als Urlaub: Eine Geschichte der Ökologie in Norwegen	26	Peder Anker, University of Oslo Science As a Vacation: A History of Ecology in Norway
62	Biografie	62	Biography
65	Impressum	65	About this publication

Severin Dünser

Eine Berggeschichte

Die Ausstellung des dänischen Künstlers Tue Greenfort verbindet eine Reihe von Geschichten aus Kunst- und Kulturproduktion, aus Ökologie und Ökonomie mit Fragen nach mittlerweile verwässerten Kategorien wie der Nachhaltigkeit und dem Naturbegriff zu einem filigranen Netz. Es überlappen sich Thematiken und filigranen Figurationen. Formaler Ausgangspunkt sind unter anderem die Geschichte und die Lokalität des Kunstraum Dornbirn, dem Greenfort eine neue räumliche Struktur einschreibt.

Es handelt sich um eine ehemalige Montagehalle. 1893 erbaut, hatte sie den Zweck, Arbeitsprozesse zu vereinfachen, auch zu rationalisieren. Ein ökonomisches Motiv, das heutzutage in einem Zug mit dem Verlust von Arbeitsplätzen genannt wird, aber eine Parallele zur Ökologie hat: Auch hier geht es darum, Ressourcen schonend einzusetzen, genauso wie bei der Kuppel, die der Künstler im Raum platziert hat. Die gegensätzlich scheinenden Motive aus Ökonomie und Ökologie treffen sich hier, werfen aber auch Fragen auf. Genauso wie der Ausstellungstitel und die Werke, die darunter versammelt sind:

Wenn man einen Berggipfel erreicht, hat man dann die Natur bezwungen oder hatte man ein Naturerlebnis? Was hat die Geschichte des Bergsteigens mit Ökologie, Hippie-Träumen und -Dystopien zu tun? Wie kann man den Auswüchsen des Kapitalismus begegnen? Durch eine Do-it-yourself-Kultur? Wo hört die Geschichte der Ökologie auf, wo beginnen die Geschichten des Rationalismus? Kann Natur nur innerhalb von Kultur verstanden werden? Wie unterläuft man Langeweile in der zeitgenössischen Kunst? Was würde Buckminster Fuller sagen? Durch eine geodätische Kuppel? Und ist diese Kuppel größer als eine Skulptur, ist sie Architektur oder eine künstlerische Intervention?

Greenfort wirft Fragen in den Raum, statt Antworten zu geben, und überlässt dem Besucher das Ziehen von Schlüssen daraus. Er stellt dabei die institutionellen Normen zeitgenössischer Kunst infrage, ebenso wie die Funktion von Kunst an sich und die damit verbundene Deutungshoheit. Es geht nicht darum, etwas Wahres, Gutes oder Schönes zu zeigen, und schon gar nicht darum, dass der Besucher etwas glauben muss. Vielmehr geht es dem Künstler um die Demokratisierung eines Erkenntnisprozesses, und damit auch um die Emanzipation des Betrachters, der sich dieser Anforderung auch stellen muss.

Greenfort versteht sich weniger als Künstler, sondern vielmehr als eine Person, die Prozesse in Gang

Severin Dünser

A Mountain Story

This exhibition of the Danish artist brings together a series of stories on the production of art and culture, on ecology and economics, and links them with questions about (meanwhile) watered-down categories such as sustainability and the concept of nature, thus weaving them into a filigree web of overlapping themes and figurations. His formal starting point is the history and locality of Kunstraum Dornbirn, which he invests with a new spatial structure.

A structure that was formerly a factory assembly hall. Built in 1893, it had the purpose of simplifying the work process and also rationalizing it. A motivating economic force that is today mentioned in one breath with the loss of workplaces, but has an aspect that parallels ecology. Namely, here too, the issue is about applying resources sparingly, exactly like the dome that the artist has placed in the room. The seemingly contrasting motives behind economics and ecology team up here, but also raise questions. Just as does the exhibition title as well as the works assembled under its mantle.

When you reach a mountaintop, have you conquered nature or had a nature experience? What does the history of mountain climbing have to do with ecology, hippie dreams and dystopias? How can we confront the excesses of capitalism? By a do-it-yourself culture? Where does the (hi)story of ecology stop and the (hi)stories of rationalism begin? Can nature only be understood within a culture? How do you undermine boredom in contemporary art? What would Buckminster Fuller say? By way of a geodesic dome? And is this dome larger than a sculpture? Is it architecture or an artistic intervention?

Greenfort throws questions into the ring instead of providing answers and leaves it to viewers to come to their own conclusions. He hereby calls the institutional norms of contemporary art in question, likewise the function of art per se and the prerogative of interpretation that is linked to it. This is not about showing something true, good or beautiful, and certainly not at all about the visitor having to believe, or go along with, something. Rather the artist is interested in the democratization of a cognitive process, and thus concerns the emancipation of the viewer who must naturally also learn to deal with this.

Greenfort doesn't see himself so much as an artist but more as a person who sets processes in

setzt und dadurch zum Nachdenken anstößt. Auch bei der zu sehenden Kuppel ist nicht klar, wie man sie definieren soll: Ist sie ein Kunstwerk von Tue Greenfort oder eine Architektur nach Buckminster Fuller? Greenfort jedenfalls platziert sie im Raum, und es stellt sich die Frage, ob es wichtig ist, ob etwas als Kunst deklariert ist, oder ob es nicht reicht, dass davon ausgehend über Dinge nachgedacht werden kann.

Wie schon kurz erwähnt, ist die Kuppel nach Plänen von Richard Buckminster Fuller gebaut. Der stellte eine 62 Meter hohe Version des „geodätische Kuppel" genannten Baus 1967 bei der Weltausstellung in Montreal aus und wurde damit schnell berühmt. Und das nicht wegen seines spektakulären Aussehens, sondern der Idee dahinter. Es ging ihm darum, mit möglichst wenig Ressourcen eine möglichst funktionale Struktur zu schaffen (der Begriff Synergieeffekt stammt übrigens auch von ihm) – die Außenfläche der Kuppel ist z.B. 40 % kleiner als sie bei einem quadratischen Gebäude mit gleicher Grundfläche wäre. Aufgegriffen wurde die Form recht schnell von den Hippies, die anfingen, ihre eigenen Kuppeln aus Wegwerfmaterialien zu bauen.

Hier verwendet Greenfort Bauplanen, wie man sie von Baustellen kennt, samt darauf gedruckter Werbung. Ähnlich der Idee der Freitag-Taschen werden diese Bauplanen recyclet und als Hülle wiederverwendet; an der Außenseite ist noch Reklame zu erkennen, die jetzt allerdings nicht mehr zu Konsum und Wegwerfen animiert, sondern im besten Fall vor Regen schützt.

Was das jetzt mit dem Bergsteigen zu tun hat? Die Erholung in der freien Natur war schon im frühen 19. Jahrhundert in Mode, der österreichische Alpenverein wurde 1862 gegründet. In weiterer Folge kam es vermehrt zu Expeditionen in höher liegende Gebiete, etwa in den Himalaya, wo man mit dort ansässigen Bergvölkern in Berührung kam. Kulturen in kargen Gebieten zeichnen sich durch einen äußerst sparsamen und effizienten Lebensstil aus. Diese Eindrücke führten unter anderem auch dazu, dass der Alpinismus sich im 20. Jahrhundert nicht mehr nur mit dem Bezwingen der Berge beschäftigte, sondern man auch anfing, sich darüber Gedanken zu machen, wie man die Natur nicht nur unberührt lassen, sondern sie auch erhalten kann. Darauf bezogen sich schließlich die Ökobewegungen, und natürlich auch die Hippies, die Buckminster Fullers Kuppeln nachbauten.

Vor der Kuppel ist ein Modell zu sehen, ebenfalls von Tue Greenfort, diesmal nach einer Leichtbau-Zeltkonstruktion von Frei Otto aus dem Jahr 1957. Auch bei *Tent* (2007) geht es darum, aus Werbeplanen funktionale Architektur herzustellen, also mittels ein paar Stangen, Seilen und Wegwerfmaterial Raum für Menschen zu schaffen.

Auch zu sehen, vielmehr jedoch zu hören, ist die Soundinstallation *Audio System* (2011). Dafür wurden

motion and triggers reflection, deliberation, cerebration. As to the dome on view, it is also not clear how it should be defined. Is it an artwork by Tue Greenfort or architecture by Buckminster Fuller? In any case Greenfort has placed it in the room, and the question gets posed as to whether it is important that something be declared art or whether it's not sufficient that, beginning from there, we can think about objects.

As already briefly mentioned, the dome was built from Richard Buckminster Fuller's plans. He exhibited a 62m-high version of the building called a "geodesic dome" in 1967 at the World's Fair in Montreal and quickly became famous. And not just because of its spectacular appearance, but for the idea behind it. He was concerned to produce the best possible functional structure with the least resources (the concept of synergetics and its effect originated with him); e.g., the exterior surface of the dome is 40 % smaller than a building with the same square base would need. The geodesic form was quickly taken up by hippies who began to build their own domes from castoff materials.

Here Greenfort uses sheets of tarpaulin such as the kind from construction sites, including the advertisements printed on them. Similar to the idea of the Friday bags, this tarpaulin is recycled and reused as covering; ads can be seen on the outside that however no longer animate us to consume and then throw away, but at the most to shield us from rain.

Now what does this have to do with climbing mountains? Recreation in nature was already in fashion in the early 19th century; the Austrian Alpine Club was founded in 1862. In a continuation, an increase in expeditions to higher regions took place, such as the Himalayas, where contact was made with the local mountain people. Cultures in barren regions are characterized by an extremely sparse and efficient lifestyle. This perception, among other things, led to the fact that alpinists in the 20th century were not just engaged in conquering the mountains but began to think not only about how to leave nature untouched, but also how to conserve it. The eco-movement built on this, and naturally the hippies who recreated Buckminster Fuller's domes.

Another model can be seen in front of the dome, also by Tue Greenfort, this time following a lightweight tent construction by Frei Otto from 1957. The point also with *Tent* (2007) is to produce functional architecture that conjures room for people out of advertising tarpaulin by means of a pair of poles, ropes and castoff material.

Also to be seen – but more to be heard – is the sound installation *Audio System* (2011), for which microphones have been installed inside and outside

Mikrofone im Innen- und Außenbereich des Kunstraums angebracht. Die Signale werden durch einen Computer geleitet. Dieser legt einen Audiofilter darüber und leitet die Signale per Zufallsgenerator wieder in den Raum, wo sich die verschiedenen Geräusche zu einem Klangteppich verweben. Natur und Menschen werden akustisch in den Raum getragen, der sonst eher von andächtiger Stille beherrscht wird.

Auch mit der Arbeit *Conservation* (2011) lässt er die Widersprüche von Natur und Museum aufeinanderprallen. Die eigentliche Aufgabe eines Museums liegt gewöhnlich darin, die ausgestellten Objekte zu erhalten und zu bewahren. Holzwürmer und ähnliche Schädlinge versucht man loszuwerden. Holz, das im Grunde ein lebendes Material ist, wird abgetötet und für die Ewigkeit vorbereitet. Ganz im Gegensatz dazu, ist das Holz, das sich bei Greenfort unter einer Glaskuppel befindet, von Holzkäfern bevölkert, und man kann dem geschützten Zerfall praktisch zuschauen: Irgendwann wird dann nur noch ein Haufen Sägemehl unter dem Glas zu sehen sein. Es geht hier also um Zeit und die natürliche Vergänglichkeit, was auch durch die formale Anlehnung an eine Standuhr suggeriert wird. Darüber hinaus ist nicht ganz klar, ob der Kunstraum auf diese Weise vor den Holzkäfern beschützt wird oder die Käfer vor den Besuchern.

Ebenfalls ein Memento Mori, aber mehr noch eine diskrete Mahnung ist die Arbeit *Untitled* (2010). In einer Flasche sind 10 Liter Alkohol, den man in kleinen Dosen entnehmen und in einer dafür vorgesehenen Schale verbrennen kann. 10 Liter, das ist der durchschnittliche Jahresverbrauch eines Österreichers, und der Becher, mit dem der Alkohol umgeschüttet werden kann, lässt uns wissen, dass man täglich 1.800 Kilokalorien zum Leben braucht, was 25,7 cl Alkohol entspricht. Vielen Menschen, etwa in der dritten Welt, steht diese Menge an Nahrung leider nicht zur Verfügung.

Tue Greenfort hat mit der Ausstellung nicht nur Dinge versammelt, sondern versucht, eine Struktur zu schaffen. Als Kunst sollen nicht die Objekte gesehen werden, sondern der Prozess. Es ist ein Projekt, das von vielen Köpfen getragen wird, nicht von Individualität. Seien es die historischen Positionen, die Mitarbeiter, Theoretiker und Philosophen, die hier ihren Teil dazu beigetragen haben, dass die Ausstellung so geworden ist, oder die Besucher selbst: Es geht darum, viele Geschichten – auch die persönlichen der Besucher – zur Interaktion zu bringen. Und darum, ein Bewusstsein dafür zu schaffen, dass man Teil einer Tradition und Geschichte ist. Die Ausstellung dreht sich folglich nicht nur um Geschichte und Geschichten, sondern versucht, selbst eine Narration, ein Prozess zu sein: eine offene, mitunter chaotische, aber dynamische Einheit, ohne abrupten Anfang oder Ende.

---

the Kunstraum. The signals are routed through a computer, which superimposes an audio filter and directs the signals per random generator back into the room where the different sounds are woven into a soundscape. Nature and people are brought into the room acoustically, which is otherwise more likely dominated by reverent silence.

Also with the work *Conservation* (2011) the artist allows the antithesis between nature and museum to cross swords. Normally the museum tries to safeguard and preserve the exhibited objects. The staff wants to get rid of woodworm and similar vermin. Wood, which is actually a living material, is deadened and made ready for eternity. Quite in contrary to the wood Greenfort uses, which is kept under a glass dome and inhabited by wood beetles, wood whose sheltered disintegration we can practically watch. At one time or other, only a pile of sawdust will remain under the glass. The issue here is time and the naturalness of transience, which also suggests a formal analogue to the hourglass. Whereby it is also not quite clear if the Kunstraum is in this way protected from the wood beetles or the beetles from the visitors.

The work *Untitled* (2010) is likewise a memento mori, but even more a discrete omen. From a bottle, 10 liters of alcohol can be withdrawn in small dosages and burnt in a bowl meant for this purpose. Ten liters: that is an Austrian's average annual consumption. And the beaker with which the alcohol is poured allows us to realize that one needs 1,800 kilokalories daily in order to live, which corresponds to 15.7 cl. of alcohol. Many people, for instance in the third world, do not have this amount of sustenance at their disposal.

With this exhibition, Tue Greenfort has not only assembled items, but tried to create a structure. The objects should not be seen as art, but as a process. This is a project that is borne by many minds, not by individuality. Whether these be the historical positions, the coworkers, theorists and philosophers that have contributed their part to the way the exhibition looks or the visitors themselves: it is about the many stories – also the visitors' personal ones – that generate the interaction. And thus creates a consciousness of the fact that one is part of a tradition and a (hi)story. And the exhibition not only revolves around history and stories, but attempts to be a narration, a process in itself: an open, at times chaotic but dynamic entity, without an abrupt beginning or end.

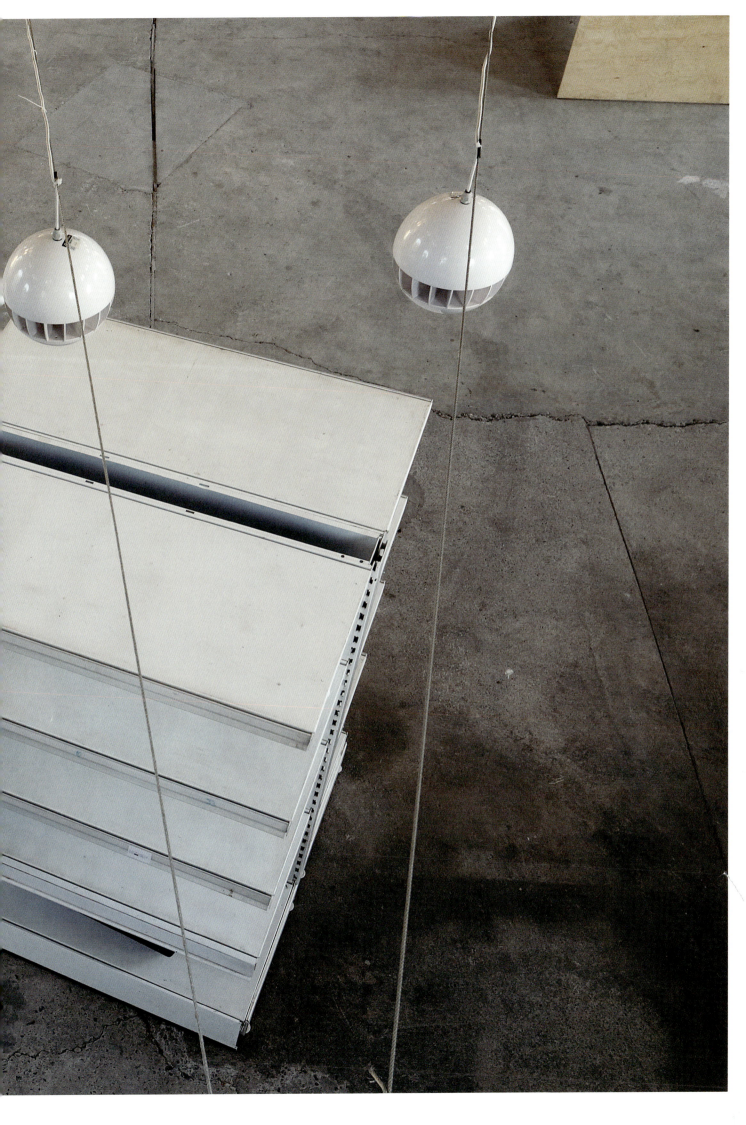

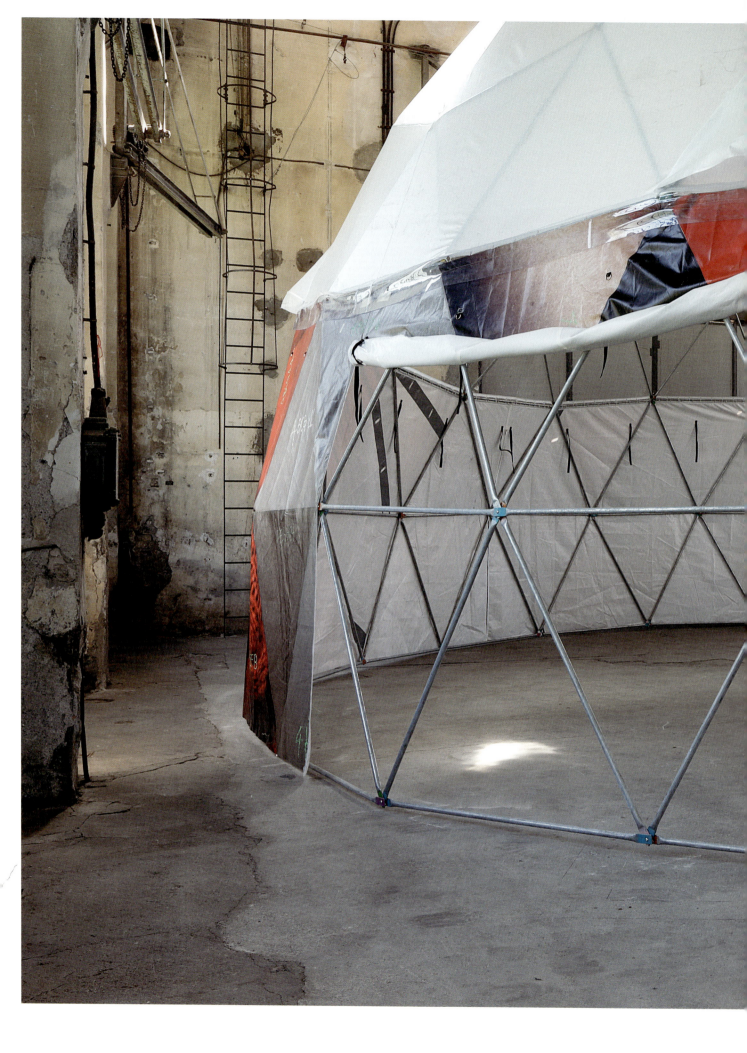

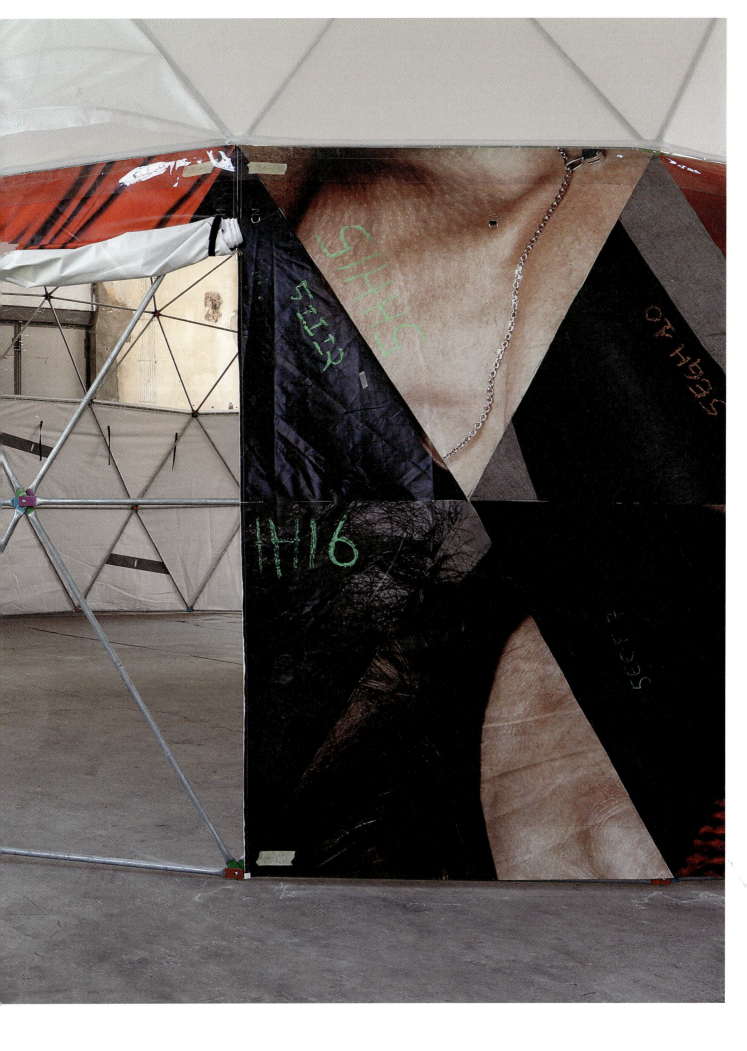

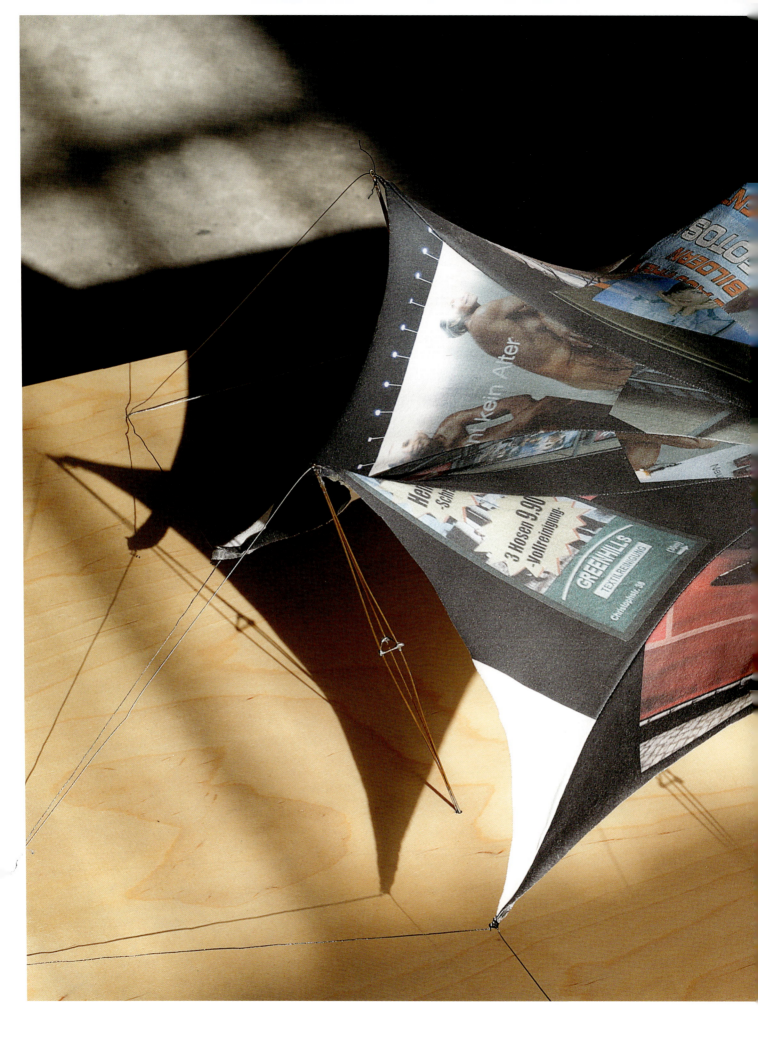

Peder Anker, Universität Oslo

Wissenschaft als Urlaub: Eine Geschichte der Ökologie in Norwegen

„Was sollen wir tun? Wie sollen wir leben?" In seiner berühmten Vorlesung *Wissenschaft als Beruf (vocation)* sagte Max Weber seinen Studenten, diese Fragen könnten und dürften Wissenschaftler nicht beantworten. Vielmehr erklärte er ihnen, dass Wissenschaft „ein fachlich betriebener ‚Beruf' ist im Dienst der Selbstbesinnung und der Erkenntnis tatsächlicher Zusammenhänge, und nicht eine Heilsgüter und Offenbarungen spendende Gnadengabe von Sehern [und] Denkern."[1] Wie ich in meinem Beitrag darlegen möchte, kam dieses Ideal einer wertfreien Wissenschaft zum Erliegen, als in den späten 1960er Jahren Studenten bei Wissenschaftlern Rat einholten, was angesichts der ökologischen Krise zu tun sei und wie man in Harmonie mit der natürlichen Welt leben könne.

Die Universität Oslo wurde zu einem einflussreichen Hort für solche ökologisch geprägten Programme und Philosophien, die der Welt raten, was zu tun und wie zu leben sei. Der Mitverfasser von *Die Grenzen des Wachstums* (1972) Jørgen Randers, der Gründer der Tiefenökologie Arne Næss, die Vorsitzende der Weltkommission für Umwelt und Entwicklung Gro Harlem Brundtland und der namhafte Friedensforscher Johan Galtung, sie alle wurden von den Osloer Ökologen in ihre Auseinandersetzungen einbezogen. Diese bislang weitgehend unbekannte Gruppe von Wissenschaftlern und Umweltaktivisten, deren innovatives Denken zur „Ökophilosophie", „Ökosophie", „Ökopolitik" und „Ökoreligion" Jahrzente lang die internationalen Debatten bestimmt hat, möchte ich an dieser Stelle eingehender beleuchten.

Wissenschaft als Urlaub (vacation) bedeutet nicht, dass die betreffenden Forscher faul gewesen wären oder ihre Aufgabe nicht ernst genommen hätten. Im Gegenteil: Sie arbeiteten hart und waren überaus engagiert. Tatsächlich führten sie wichtige Teile ihrer Forschungen durch, während man sie auf Erholungsurlaub wähnte, da Felderkundungen im Gebirge sich mitunter nur im kurzen semi-arktischen Sommer bewerkstelligen ließen. In Anbetracht dieses Phänomens möchte ich zeigen, dass die ökologischen Wissenschaften in Norwegen aus einer Kultur erwuchsen, in der Natur nicht als Arbeitsplatz, sondern als Raum für Freilandurlaub aufgefasst wurde.[2] Mehr noch: Indem diese Ökologen eine soziale und

Peder Anker, University of Oslo

Science As a Vacation: A History of Ecology in Norway

"What should we do? How should we live?" In his famous lecture, *Science As a Vocation*, Max Weber told his students that scientists could and should not provide answers. Instead, he told them to look at science as "a 'vocation' conducted through specialist disciplines to serve the cause of reflection on the self and knowledge of relationships between facts, not a gift of grace from seers and prophets dispensing sacred values and revelations".[1] This ideal of a value-free science came to a standstill, as this article will argue, when students of the late 1960s demanded advice from scientists on what to do with the ecological crisis and how to live in harmony with the natural world.

The University of Oslo became an influential hotbed for such ecologically informed policies and philosophies advising the world about what to do and how to live. The co-author of *The Limits of Growth* (1972) Jørgen Randers, the founder of Deep Ecology Arne Næss, the Chair of the World Commission on Environment and Development Gro Harlem Brundtland, and the famed peace researcher Johan Galtung, were all engaged by the Oslo ecologists. This article will describe in some detail this hitherto largely unknown group of scientists and environmental activists, as their innovative thinking about "ecophilosophy", "ecosophy", "eco-politics", and "eco-religion" came to dominate international debates for decades.

Science as a vacation does not mean that these scholars were lazy or did not take their work seriously. On the contrary: they were hardworking, committed scholars. Indeed, much of their research was carried out while they were supposed to be on vacation, as some of the mountain fieldwork could be done only during the short semi-arctic summer. What I propose instead is that ecological sciences in Norway grew out of a culture in which nature was understood not as a place of work but in terms of outdoor vacationing.[2] Moreover, by taking a social and political stand on environmental questions, these ecologists came to oppose the value-free way of practising science. Thus science as a vacation suggests the opposite of Weber's vocation ideals. Furthermore, the Protestant work ethic and the spirit of capitalism Weber once described represented the very industrial horror Norwegian ecologists believed caused the environmental havoc of our age. Finally, science as a vacation addresses the calling for a

politische Haltung zu Umweltfragen einnahmen, stellten sie sich letztlich der Auffassung von einer wertfreien Wissenschaftspraxis entgegen. Wissenschaft als Urlaub bedeutet demnach das Gegenteil von Webers Berufsidealen. Darüber hinaus standen die protestantische Arbeitsethik und der Geist des Kapitalismus, die Weber einst beschrieb, für eben das industrielle Grauen, das nach Überzeugung der norwegischen Ökologen die verheerenden Umweltschäden unseres Zeitalters verursachte. Und schließlich folgt Wissenschaft als Urlaub dem Ruf nach einer neuen Ökophilosophie zum Thema, was in freier Wildbahn zu tun und wie dort zu leben sei. „Die Kathederpropethie wird vollends nur fanatische Sekten, aber nie eine echte [wissenschaftliche] Gemeinschaft schaffen"[3], warnte Weber. Hatte er Recht?

Weber hatte von der wissenschaftlichen Gemeinschaft ein einbezügliches Verständnis, das den gesamten Corpus akademischer Forschung umschloss. Ebenso umfassend möchte ich in diesem Beitrag die fachübergreifende ökologische Debatte an der Universität Oslo erörtern, von der man übrigens kaum behaupten kann, dass sie in „zwei Kulturen" gespalten gewesen sei.[4] Besonders intensiv verliefen die sozialen Interaktionen zwischen Ökologen und Philosophen von 1966 bis Herbst 1972; danach verlagerte sich die Umweltdiskussion großenteils nach außerhalb des Campus. In diese Zeit fielen die Gründerjahre der Tiefenökologie in Oslo; was dabei geschah, ist bei Historikern, die sich mit Ökologie und Umweltdebatten beschäftigen, weithin unbeachtet geblieben.[5] Ebenso haben die Wissenschaftshistoriker im Allgemeineren die Bedeutung der Ferien für die wissenschaftliche Forschung übersehen, obwohl doch die drei besten Momente im akademischen Leben bekanntlich die Monate Juni, Juli und August sind.

Auf den folgenden Seiten möchte ich zunächst die norwegische Urlaubskultur beleuchten und die Ökologen und Umweltphilosophen in diesem Zusammenhang verorten. Im nächsten Abschnitt erörtere ich die Aktivitäten von Ökologen, insbesondere von Wissenschaftlern, die sich im Internationalen Biologischen Programm (IBP) betätigt haben. Ihre Sorge um die Zukunft der Umwelt hat viele Studenten und aktivistische Philosophen dazu bewogen, die Bedingungen des Menschen in der natürlichen Welt neu zu bedenken – Überlegungen, die in den abschließenden Teilen im Blickpunkt stehen.

Die Kultur des Freilandurlaubs

In den 1960er Jahren wurden viele Häuser der schwindenden Klasse hart arbeitender Fjord- und Bergbauern von Urlaubern gekauft, die ihre Freizeit mit tradierten Betätigungen ländlichen Stils ausfüllen wollten. Dieses Phänomen reihte sich ein in den Trend zur Freilanderholung in den reizvollsten Gegenden der Nation, durch den die Natur sich vom Arbeitsplatz zum Freizeitgelände wandelte. Tausende

new eco-philosophy about what do to and how to live in the wild. Weber warned that such "academic prophecy will create only fanatical sects, never a true [scientific] community".[3] Was he right?

Weber had an inclusive view of the scientific community, encompassing the entire body of academic research. This article will be equally broad in discussing the interdisciplinary ecological debate at the University of Oslo which was hardly divided by "two cultures".[4] The social interactions were particularly intense between ecologists and philosophers from 1966 until the autumn of 1972, after which much of the environmental debate moved off-campus. The formative years of deep ecology took place in this period in Oslo, in events that historians of ecology and environmental debates have largely ignored.[5] Equally overlooked among historians of science more generally has been the importance of vacations to scientific research, despite the well-known fact that the three best aspects of academic life are June, July, and August.

The following pages will first lay out the Norwegian culture of vacation and situate the ecologists and the environmental philosophers within this context. The next section will discuss the activities of ecologists, especially of scholars active in the International Biological Program (IBP). Their concerns for the environmental future mobilized a series of students and activist philosophers to rethink the human condition in the natural world, reasoning that will be the focus of the final sections.

The culture of outdoor vacation

In the 1960s many of the homes of the vanishing class of hardworking Norwegian fjord and mountain farmers were bought by vacationers seeking to fill their leisuretime with country-style activities of the past. This phenomenon was part of a boom in outdoor recreation in the nation's most scenic places, which turned nature from a place of work into a place of leisure. Thousands of cottages were built in the mountains and by the fjords to satisfy back-to-nature lovers seeking harmony with their holiday environment. By 1970 fifteen percent of a total of 3.7 million Norwegians had their own private vacation homes, totalling 190,000 cottages. And the numbers were growing radically, as a quarter of these places were built after 1965. The overwhelming majority of Norwegians did not have their own vacation home, but surveys show that they either borrowed or rented a cottage, or stayed in hostels, or sports hotels.[6] Indeed, in 1970 only sixteen percent of the population did not participate in some sort of outdoor recreation, and this group consisted mostly of the elderly. Despite imagined and real precursors back in history, this cult of outdoor life was a new

von Ferienhäusern wurden in den Bergen und an den Fjords gebaut, um Menschen zu bedienen, die unter dem Motto „Zurück zur Natur" nach Harmonie mit ihrer Ferienumwelt strebten. Um 1970 besaßen 15 Prozent der 3,7 Millionen Norweger ein eigenes Urlaubsdomizil, 190.000 Ferienhäuser insgesamt. Und deren Zahl stieg rapide an, war doch ein Viertel dieser Unterkünfte erst nach 1965 entstanden. In ihrer großen Mehrheit hatten die Norweger zwar nach wie vor kein Ferien-Eigenheim, doch belegen Statistiken, dass die meisten sich ein Ferienhaus liehen oder mieteten oder aber in Herbergen und Sporthotels logierten.[6] So nahmen 1970 nur 16 Prozent der Bevölkerung nicht an irgendeiner Art von Freilanderholung teil, und diese Gruppe bestand größtenteils aus älteren Menschen. Trotz imaginierter und realer geschichtlicher Vorläufer war der Kult um das Freilandleben ein neues Phänomen, das den wachsenden Wohlstand der Nation widerspiegelte.[7] Das Urlaubswesen wuchs zu einer ansehnlichen Industrie heran und brachte eigene Interessensgruppen hervor, die für die Umwelt als Freizeitgelände eintraten. Die Kämpfe für den Aufbau von Nationalparks, die zwischen der Eröffnung des ersten Parks im Jahr 1962 und der Einrichtung mehrerer Parks im Jahr 1971 erheblich zunahmen, zeugen von der steigenden Macht der Tourismusbranche. Zur gleichen Zeit nahmen Entwicklungen auf dem Gebiet der Wasserkraft und andere Landschaftsmodernisierungen Gestalt an. Was die Flächenbeanspruchung betrifft, hatten dabei der Freilandurlaub und der Ferienhäuserbau weitaus einschneidendere Auswirkungen als die Errichtung neuer Dämme, auch wenn sie nicht ganz so geballt daherkamen. Da indes massive Dämme den Urlaubern nicht ins Konzept passten, war ein Interessenskonflikt letztlich unvermeidlich.

Die Gründungsjahre der ökologischen Forschung in Norwegen fielen genau in diese Zeit und dieses Umfeld, und das diesbezügliche Verständnis der Ökologen widerspiegelte denn auch ihr Erleben der Natur als Urlaubsgebiet. Sie wurden zu mächtigen Lobbyisten groß angelegter Nationalparks, sodass den künftigen Ferienhausbesitzern und Touristen die von ihnen favorisierte Natur sicher sein würde. Häufig argumentierte man, die Nähe zur unberührten Natur sei für die Gesundheit unerlässlich. Der Ökologe Eilif Dahl (1916–93) zum Beispiel sah in urbanen sozialen Problemen eine Folge mangelnden Naturkontakts. Menschen hätten ein emotionales „Bedürfnis nach Erfüllung", behauptete er, das sich nur durch „Begegnungen mit der Natur"[8] befriedigen lasse. Viele seiner Kollegen waren ähnlicher Ansicht. Ein Leben ohne Freilandurlaub könne zu gefährlichen städtischen „Ghetto"-Kulturen führen, weil Menschen „Erholung brauchen, und zwar zunehmend Erholung im Kontakt mit der Natur".[9]

Die Spitzeneinrichtung für ökologische Forschung in Norwegen war die 1965 in Finse gegründete High

phenomenon reflecting the growing wealth of the nation.[7] Vacationing grew into a sizeable industry with its own interest groups defending the environment as a place of leisure. The battles to create national parks, which grew in intensity between the creation of the first park in 1962 and the establishment of a series of parks in 1971, bear witness to the growing power of the tourism business. At the same time, various hydro-power developments and other modernizations of the landscape took shape. In terms of pressure on the land, outdoor vacationing and the building of cottages had a far more radical effect than the building of new dams, though its impact was not as centralized. Since large dams did not match vacationers' agenda, a conflict of interest was eventually inevitable.

The formative years of ecological research in Norway took place in this period and in these environments, and the way ecologists came to understand it would reflect their experience of nature as a place of vacation. They became powerful lobbyists in favour of large-scale national parks so that cottage owners and tourists of the future were secured the nature they enjoyed the most. They would frequently argue that being in proximity with untouched nature was necessary for health. The ecologist Eilif Dahl (1916–93), for example, saw urban social problems as a result of lack of contact with nature. Humans have an emotional "need to thrive", he argued, which can be satisfied only through "meetings with nature".[8] Many of his colleagues agreed. Life without outdoor vacation could lead to dangerous urban "ghetto" cultures, since humans "demand recreation, and increasingly recreation in contact with nature".[9]

The chief place to do ecological research in Norway was The High Mountain Ecology Research Station established at Finse in 1965. Finse is a railway station halfway between Oslo and Bergen, located at the very heart of outdoor recreational activities. Turn-of-the-century dwellings of 'navvy' railway maintainers were here turned into high-end vacation homes, side by side with a well-known sports hotel, a large hospice owned by the Norwegian Trekking Association, and numerous new private cabins. Here thousands of vacationers would enjoy one of the most beautiful mountain regions of Norway. It was the zoologists Arne Semb-Johansson (1919–2001) and Eivind Østbye (b. 1935) who created the Research Station with financial support from the University of Oslo. Following the trend of the area, they turned an outdated power-station into a cabin for research and teaching of graduates.[10] Ecology was at the time a new discipline in Norway.[11] The first lectures on the subject were given by Semb-Johansson and Østbye at the University of Oslo in 1962 and by Dahl at the Norwegian Agricultural College in 1963. These courses

Mountain Ecology Research Station. Finse ist ein Bahnhof auf halber Strecke zwischen Oslo und Bergen und liegt mitten in einem Gebiet für Freiland-Erholungsaktivitäten. Aus der Jahrhundertwende stammende Unterkünfte für angelerntes Eisenbahnwartungspersonal wurden dort zu edlen Urlaubsdomizilen umgebaut; ein bekanntes Sporthotel, ein großes Gästehaus im Besitz des norwegischen Wandervereins und zahlreiche neue private Katen befinden sich in der Nähe. Tausende von Urlaubern genießen hier eine von Norwegens schönsten Gebirgsgegenden. Gegründet wurde die Station von den Zoologen Arne Semb-Johansson (1919–2001) und Eivind Østbye (geb. 1935) mit finanzieller Unterstützung der Universität Oslo. Dem lokalen Trend entsprechend, widmeten sie ein ausgedientes Kraftwerk zu einem Haus der Forschung und Lehre für Hochschulabsolventen um.[10] Ökologie war damals in Norwegen ein neues Fach.[11] Die ersten Vorlesungen zum Thema hatten Semb-Johansson und Østbye 1962 an der Universität Oslo und Dahl 1963 an der Norwegischen Hochschule für Agrarwirtschaft gehalten. Sie behandelten die Energiekreisläufe in der Natur, wie sie der amerikanische Ökologe Eugene P. Odum (1913–2002) beschrieben hatte.[12] Dessen Methodik war richtungsweisend für die norwegische ökologische Forschung, die sich auf das Energiegleichgewicht zwischen Arten spezialisierte. Insbesondere galt das für Wissenschaftler, die von Finse aus arbeiteten, wo Semb-Johansson und Østbye ihre Kurse gaben. Dabei erlebte das neue Fachgebiet einen erheblichen Aufschwung, da die biotischen Beziehungen in der Gebirgswelt unkomplizierter als im Flachland sind und sich deshalb vergleichsweise leichter lehren und untersuchen lassen.[13]

Die Sommerexkursionen in die malerischen Berge von Finse waren sehr beliebt, gaben sie doch Studenten wie Wissenschaftlern das Gefühl, in der vorlesungsfreien Sommerzeit etwas gleichermaßen Nützliches und Angenehmes zu tun. Auch wenn die persönliche Motivation von Ökologen schwer zu bestimmen ist, kann man mit Sicherheit sagen, dass die meisten Studenten, die sich auf dieses Gebiet begaben, eine Leidenschaft für Freilanderholung hatten. Bezeichnenderweise war es für sie mehrheitlich eine Selbstverständlichkeit, dem über 60.000 Mitglieder zählenden Wanderverein beizutreten, der der größte Eigentümer von Ferienhäusern im Lande ist. Über 800 Forschungstage haben Studenten und Wissenschaftler zwischen 1965 und 1970 in der Forschungsstation durchgeführt. Größtenteils wirkten sie in der norwegischen Sektion des Internationalen Biologischen Programms mit; einige lebten auch ganzjährig in Finse, um die ökologischen Verhältnisse im strengen Winter zu untersuchen (von dem übrigens die vor Ort gedrehten Kampfszenen des Films *Das Imperium schlägt zurück*, 1979, ein Bild vermitteln). 1970 bewilligte das norwegische Parla-

were devoted to energy circulations in nature as this was described by the American ecologist Eugene P. Odum (1913–2002).[12] This methodology dominated Norwegian ecological research, which came to focus on the energy balance between species. This was especially the case with scholars working out of Finse where Semb-Johansson and Østbye would give their courses. This brought significant momentum to the field, as it was easier to teach and study relatively uncomplicated biotic relations of the mountains in comparison with lowland environments.[13]

The summer excursions to the scenic mountains of Finse were very popular, as they gave students and scholars alike a sense of doing something useful and pleasant during their summer recess. Though it is hard to determine the personal motivation of ecologists, it is safe to say that most students entering the field had a passion for outdoor recreation. Typically, membership in the Trekking Association, the nation's largest owner of cottages with over sixty thousand members, was to most of them a matter of course. Over eight hundred days of research were carried out by students and scholars at the Research Station between 1965 and 1970. Most of them were involved in the Norwegian division of the International Biological Program, and a few of them lived at Finse on a yearly basis to study the ecology of harsh winters (captured in the Hoth battle-scenes of *The Empire Strikes Back* (1979) which were shot there). In 1970 the Norwegian Parliament allocated enough funds to build a new 700 m² building to be owned jointly by the Universities of Oslo and Bergen. When finished in 1972 it was, perhaps, the largest and most expensive ecological research station in Europe. It could house large courses, which were usually given in August. The historian of science Robert E. Kohler has in his study of fieldwork in the U.S. noted that "[t]he most widespread form of underwriting [of field work] was the summer vacation, which all academics and most government and museum employees enjoyed. Vacations afforded not money but time".[14] This was also very much the case for Oslo ecologists, whose long summer recess enabled them to do their field work as the nature in question was easily accessible during this period. This scientific vacationing was not necessarily relaxing, although anecdotal evidence suggests that for some it was that too. Hardworking or not, fieldwork was the highlight of the year as it enabled ecologists to spent time in places they appreciated as and associated with outdoor life.

Finse was also the site for large archaeological excavations of Stone Age hunting and gathering culture. For the ecologists as well as many ordinary vacationers, this remembrance of things past came to represent the ability of a pre-industrial society to live self-sufficiently. One nature writer typically ob-

ment die Gelder für einen 700 qm großen Neubau, der ins gemeinschaftliche Eigentum der Universitäten Oslo und Bergen überging. 1972 fertiggestellt, beherbergte er die vielleicht größte und teuerste ökologische Forschungsstation in Europa. Er bot reichlich Platz für die stark frequentierten Kurse, die meist im August abgehalten wurden. Der Wissenschaftshistoriker Robert E. Kohler bemerkt in seiner Studie über Feldforschung in den USA, dass „die meistgewählte Einschreibungsperiode [für Feldforschungen] in den Sommerferien lag, die allen Akademikern und den meisten Regierungs- und Museumsangestellten zustanden. Ferien brachten kein Geld, aber Zeit."[14] Weitgehend galt dies auch für die Ökologen aus Oslo, die ihre Feldforschungen in der langen Sommerpause unternehmen konnten, zumal in dieser Jahreszeit die zu untersuchende Natur leicht zugänglich war. Entspannend waren solche wissenschaftlichen Urlaubsaufenthalte nicht unbedingt, auch wenn anekdotische Aussagen darauf hindeuten, dass sie dies für manche durchaus auch waren. Ob mit harter Arbeit verbunden oder nicht, die Feldforschung war der Höhepunkt des Jahres, erlaubte sie doch den Ökologen, Zeit an Orten zu verbringen, die sie mit dem Freilandleben in Verbindung brachten und als solche zu schätzen wussten.

Finse war auch eine große Ausgrabungsstätte steinzeitlicher Jäger- und Sammlerkultur. Die Ökologen, aber auch viele normale Urlauber sahen sich durch diese Dinge aus der Vergangenheit an die Selbstversorgungsfähigkeit vorindustrieller Gesellschaften erinnert. Ein Naturschriftsteller bemerkte bezeichnenderweise, das Freilandleben sei eine „partielle Rückkehr zum Naturzustand", weswegen Urlauber, die sonst in modernen Häusern wohnen, „unter freiem Himmel kochen" und „wochenlang in Zelten" leben, um mit der Steinzeit Verbindung aufzunehmen.[15]

Viele Ökologen besuchten den Philosophen Arne Næss (geb. 1912), der sich eingehend für Umweltforschung interessierte und lange Zeiten des Jahres in seiner Berghütte auf dem unweit von Finse gelegenen Hallingskarvet-Hochplateau verbrachte.[16] Næss zählte zu den Wegbereitern urwüchsigen Wohnens und hatte seine Hütte bereits 1937 gebaut, um die Natur über längere Zeiträume genießen und sich im technischen Klettern üben zu können. Berggipfel zu bezwingen war bis zu den frühen 1970er Jahren seine größte Lebensleidenschaft, und seine engsten Freunde gehörten dem norwegischen Alpenverein an. Dieser Verein war – und ist noch immer – der vielleicht exklusivste unter zahllosen Freilanderholungsgesellschaften. Der Wahlspruch „Bergsteigen verhält sich zu anderen Sportarten wie Champagner zu Bier", popularisiert durch den unter Bergsteigern viel gelesenen Naturphilosophen Peter Wessel Zapffe (1899–1990), trifft sehr schön den Geist dieser Hautevolee-Bruderschaft.[17] Legendärstes Mitglied des Clubs war jedoch Næss, der schon vor seinem

served that outdoor life was a "partial return to the state of nature" in which vacationers with modern houses choose to "cook in the open air" and live in "tents for weeks" to touch base with the Stone Age within.[15]

Many of the ecologists would visit the philosopher Arne Næss (b. 1912), who had a keen interest in ecological research and lived long periods of the year at his mountain cabin at the top of the Hallingskarvet peak near Finse.[16] He was a cottager pioneer, building his cabin back in 1937 so that he could have more time to enjoy nature and practise technical climbing. Conquering mountaintops was until the early 1970s his chief passion in life, and his closest friends were members of the Norwegian Alpine Club. The Club was – and still is – perhaps the most exclusive of a myriad of outdoor recreation societies. Their saying, "Climbing is to other sports like champagne to bock beer" – popularized by the nature philosopher Peter Wessel Zapffe (1899–1990) – captures well the spirit of this upper crust fraternity, as his essays were widely read among the climbers.[17] It was Næss, however, who was the Club's most legendary member, having ascended over one hundred of the highest mountains in Norway before his eighteenth birthday.

Practical know-how about outdoor vacations, especially technical climbing, was not a matter of course. To train Norwegians in the art Nils Faarlund (b. 1937) established The Norwegian Mountaineering School in 1967, while at the same time lecturing in Oslo at the Norwegian School of Sport Sciences from its inauguration in 1968. He had a graduate degree in engineering and biochemistry, was trained in landscape architecture and ecology in Hanover, a member of the Alpine Club and an admirer of Næss, with interests drifting towards philosophy. His school and lectures became legendary among environmentalists seeking a combination of philosophical training and practical experience in dealing with the wild. He saw "outdoor life as a means to pursue scientific research", and ecologists took him seriously by sending students in need of courses in everything from tenting and outdoor cooking to survival strategies in harsh winter climate to his School.[18] This type of knowledge was important for carrying out research in the field. To Faarlund being "outside" was actually being "inside", as nature was the only true human home. Following this line of reasoning, he formulated his own philosophy of "free-air-life" of the "free-air-person", thinking that inspired not only Næss, but the inner circle of Norway's most devoted young mountaineers and environmentally concerned ecologists.[19]

This group was centred around Sigmund Kvaløy (b. 1934), a childhood friend of Faarlund and stu-

18. Geburtstag über Hundert der höchsten Berge Norwegens erklommen hatte.

Praktische Kenntnisse im Freilandurlauben, zumal im technischen Klettern, waren keine Selbstverständlichkeit. Um die Norweger in dieser Kunst auszubilden, gründete Nils Faarlund (geb. 1937) 1967 die Norwegische Bergsteigerschule und unterrichtete daneben auch an der 1968 eingeweihten Sporthochschule in Oslo. Er hatte einen akademischen Abschluss in Ingenieurwesen und Biochemie, hatte in Hannover Landschaftsarchitektur und Ökologie gelernt, war Mitglied des Alpenvereins und Bewunderer von Næss und interessierte sich zusehends für Philosophie. Bald genossen seine Schule und seine Vorlesungen einen sagenhaften Ruf bei den Umweltschützern, die nach einer Kombination aus philosophischer Ausbildung und praktischer Erfahrung in freier Wildbahn suchten. Faarlund begriff „Freilandleben als Mittel wissenschaftlichen Forschens", und da die Ökologen ihn ernstnahmen, schickten sie Studenten, die Kurse in allem Möglichen, vom Zelten und Freiluftkochen bis zu Überlebensstrategien im rauen Winterklima brauchten, in seine Schule.[18] Derlei Wissen war wichtig für die Durchführung von Feldforschungen. Nach Faarlund hieß „draußen" zu sein eigentlich „drinnen" zu sein, denn die Natur sei das einzige wahre Heim des Menschen. Diesem Gedankengang folgend, entwickelte er seine eigene Philosophie vom „Freiluftleben" des „Freiluftmenschen", ein Denken, das nicht nur Næss inspirierte, sondern auch den inneren Kreis von Norwegens eifrigsten jungen Bergsteigern und umweltbewussten Ökologen.[19]

Diese Gruppe scharte sich um Sigmund Kvaløy (geb. 1934), einen Freund Faarlunds von Kindheit an und Studenten von Næss. Kvaløy wuchs im malerischen Bergdorf Lom auf und wurde später Bordmechaniker bei der norwegischen Luftwaffe. Seine Hauptinteressensgebiete waren Bergsteigen, Philosophie und Jazz. Seit 1961 Assistent bei Næss, schrieb er 1965 unter dessen Mentorschaft eine Magisterarbeit und erhielt ab 1967 ein vierjähriges Promotionsstipendium, das er darauf verwandte, das ökologische Denken am Zoologischen Institut zu erkunden.[20] Als aktive Mitglieder des Alpenvereins versuchten Kvaløy, Faarlund und Næss, die Ökologen des Instituts für die norwegische Tradition des Freilandlebens zu begeistern.

Ökologen als Anwälte einer erholsamen Natur

In *Wissenschaft als Beruf* erklärte Weber seinen Studenten, dass, „wo immer der Mann der Wissenschaft mit seinem eigenen Werturteil kommt, das volle Verstehen der Tatsachen aufhört".[21] Dass von Werturteilen gefärbte Tatsachen einen geringeren wissenschaftlichen Wert haben, akzeptierten auch die Osloer Ökologen, die große Mühe darauf verwandten, Pflanzen und Tiere sowie deren Beziehungen untereinander und zur Umwelt in neutralen

---

dent of Næss. Kvaløy grew up in the picturesque mountain village of Lom before becoming an air mechanic for the Norwegian Air Force. His chief interests were mountain climbing, philosophy, and jazz. As an assistant to Næss from 1961, he wrote an M.A. thesis under his supervision in 1965, and was granted a four year Ph.D. scholarship in philosophy starting in 1967, which he used to explore ecological thinking at the Department of Zoology.[20] As active members of the Alpine Club, Kvaløy, Faarlund, and Næss sought to energize the Norwegian tradition of outdoor life among the Department's ecologists.

Ecologists as advocates of a recreational nature

In *Science As a Vocation* Weber told his students that "whenever a man of science brings in his own value-judgement, a full understanding of facts ceases".[21] That facts tainted by value-judgements were of lesser scientific value was accepted also by Oslo ecologists, who used much effort to describe plants, animals, and their relations to each other and to the environment in neutral terms. Nevertheless, ecological research questions, researchers, and research results were far from neutral as they were all explicitly pointing towards conservation and recreational values.[22]

Ecological research gathered momentum in Norway through the International Biological Program, which was active between 1964 and 1974, though fully in effect only between 1967 and 1972. Nationally, altogether 221 students and scholars were connected to this Program, of whom 94 were at the University of Oslo. They were typically involved for from two to four years, and they were for the most part working on ecological topics. Housing all the new scientists was an issue, and the Parliament allocated enough funds to build a new Institute of Biology. When it was finished in 1971, it was the largest building ever built by the Norwegian state – covering 25,000m² – and it came in addition to the new Research Station at Finse. This was part of a larger state commitment to science, as the average scientific research budget in Norway increased nominally 119 % between 1963 and 1969. The biologists' share was a 186 % increase plus new buildings, all of which is evidence of substantial political support for the biological sciences.[23]

What stimulated members of the Parliament as well as the biologists was environmental concerns abroad. Rachel Carson's famous warning against pesticides in *Silent Spring* (1962), for example, raised eyebrows and inspired Norwegians to adopt an ecological perspective.[24] Equally important were the environmental writings of Lynn White, Jaques Yves Cousteau, and an essay about technological standardization of human life and nature by the Finnish

Begriffen zu beschreiben. Dennoch waren die ökologischen Forschungsziele und -ergebnisse wie auch die Forscher selbst von Neutralität weit entfernt, richteten sie sich doch allesamt ausdrücklich nach Werten der Erhaltung und der Erholung.[22]

Die ökologische Forschung bekam in Norwegen Auftrieb durch das Internationale Biologische Programm, das zwischen 1964 und 1974 lief, aber nur von 1967 bis 1972 in vollem Umfang betrieben wurde. Insgesamt waren dem Programm landesweit 221 Studenten und Wissenschaftler angeschlossen, darunter 94 von der Universität Oslo. Üblicherweise beteiligten sie sich für zwei bis vier Jahre und arbeiteten dabei größtenteils an ökologischen Themen. All die neuen Wissenschaftler unterzubringen, wurde zum Problem, weshalb das Parlament dem Institut für Biologie die Gelder für einen Neubau bewilligte. Dieser war bei seiner Fertigstellung im Jahr 1971 mit einer Fläche von 25.000 qm das größte je vom norwegischen Staat errichtete Gebäude und ergänzte die neue Forschungsstation in Finse. Die Maßnahme war übrigens Bestandteil eines umfassenderen staatlichen Engagements für die Wissenschaften: Das durchschnittliche Budget für die wissenschaftliche Forschung in Norwegen stieg zwischen 1963 und 1969 um nominell 119 %. Den Biologen kam dabei ein Zuwachs von 186 Prozent plus neuen Gebäuden zugute, was eine erhebliche politische Unterstützung für die Biowissenschaften anzeigt.[23]

Motiviert wurden Parlamentsangehörige wie Biologen von Umweltbelangen im Ausland. Beispielsweise sorgte die berühmte Warnung vor Pestiziden, die Rachel Carson in Der stumme Frühling (Silent Spring, 1962) ausgab, für beunruhigtes Stirnrunzeln und veranlasste die Norweger dazu, eine ökologische Sichtweise einzunehmen.[24] Ebenso bedeutsam waren die Umweltschriften von Lynn White, Jacques Yves Cousteau und ein Essay des finnischen Philosophen George Henrik von Wright über die technologische Standardisierung des menschlichen Lebens und der Natur. Norwegens ökologische Anliegen waren demnach anfangs importiert. Zu den ersten, die diese Anliegen in Norwegen vortrugen, gehörte Rolf Vik (1917–99), Professor für Zoologie an der Universität Oslo und Vorsitzender des Internationalen Biologischen Programms in Norwegen. Er argumentierte, bei ausreichender Finanzierung könnten die Ökologen Antworten auf die von Carson und Wright beschriebenen Umweltprobleme liefern. „Das Schlüsselwort lautet Geld", beschied er den Politikern.[25]

Diese und ähnliche Aussagen waren ausschlaggebend für den Antrag an das norwegische Parlament, Mittel für einen norwegischen Zweig des Internationalen Biologischen Programms bereitzustellen. Das Programm – das ist der Erinnerung wert – wurde 1960 von Mitgliedern der Internationalen Union der biologischen Wissenschaften sowie des Internatio-

philosopher George Henrik von Wright. Norwegian ecological concerns were thus initially imported. One of the first to bring these concerns to Norway was Rolf Vik (1917–99), a professor of zoology at the University of Oslo and chairman of the International Biological Program in Norway. He argued that ecologists could provide answers to environmental problems described by Carson and von Wright, if they were provided with enough funding. "The key word is money!", he told the politicians.[25]

These and other similar statements were central to the application to the Norwegian Parliament for funding for a Norwegian branch of the International Biological Program. This Program, it is worth recalling, was initiated in 1960 by members of the International Union of Biological Sciences and the International Council of Scientific Unions. Its main concerns were problems related to food production and management of natural resources in view of a rapidly increasing human population and widespread malnutrition. It was a 'Big Science' project and of key importance to the promotion of systems ecology driven by the image of the world as a manageable self-governing machine.[26] The managerial benefit of ecological research was, at least initially, at the heart of the Program in Norway. There were reasons to worry about food supply, because of the increasing population both at home and abroad. The ecologists pledged to deliver "methods that enable us to predict the consequences of today's actions and tomorrow's world" with respect to the utilization of the land.[27] It was "a matter of continuing human existence" to research the ecology of the mountains as future "production and recreation areas" for Norwegians.[28] One should therefore train more ecologists, the Parliament was told, with the ability to deal with problems of productivity, food production, and rational management of the nation's natural resources. To study the mountain regions was especially important, since more than half the country is situated above the tree line. As the prosperity of the nation was at stake, the Parliament voted in favour of a generous budget to train ecologists in scientific tools for landscape management.

To receive funding through the Parliament was rather unusual and it caused tensions among biologists, as applications were supposed to go through the Norwegian Research Council. The botanist Knut Fægri (1909–2001), for example, complained that ecology had become "a nice word that rumbles well in pretty reports to the Parliament and other authorities.... But do they have a clue about what they are doing?".[29] What worried Fægri was funding at the expense of taxonomy, and whether or not the ecologists could deliver what they promised. His concerns were not without foundation, as taxonomy from now

nalen Wissenschaftsrats gestartet. Hauptsächlich befasst es sich mit Problemen der Nahrungsproduktion und des Haushaltens mit natürlichen Ressourcen angesichts einer rasch ansteigenden Weltbevölkerung und weit verbreiteter Unterernährung. Das Großforschungsprojekt war von entscheidender Bedeutung für die Förderung der Systemökologie, die vom Verständnis der Welt als einer selbststeuernden, aber bewirtschaftbaren Maschine ausgeht.[26] Der Bewirtschaftungsgewinn aus ökologischer Forschung stand in Norwegen zumindest anfangs im Kern des Programms. Die Nahrungsmittelversorgung bot wegen der wachsenden Bevölkerung im In- und Ausland Anlass zur Beunruhigung. Hier versprachen die Ökologen die Bereitstellung von „Methoden, die uns in die Lage versetzen", hinsichtlich der Landnutzung „die Folgen heutigen Handelns und die Welt von morgen" vorherzusagen".[27] Es war eine Frage „des Fortbestands der menschlichen Existenz", die Ökologie der Berge als zukünftige „Produktions- und Erholungsgebiete" für die Norweger zu erforschen.[28] Deshalb sollten mehr Ökologen ausgebildet werden, sagte man dem Parlament, die mit Problemen der Produktivität, der Nahrungsmittelerzeugung und der rationellen Bewirtschaftung der Naturressourcen des Landes umgehen könnten. Die Bergregionen zu untersuchen, war besonders wichtig, weil über die Hälfte des Landes oberhalb der Baumgrenze liegt. Da der Wohlstand der Nation auf dem Spiel stand, stimmte das Parlament einem großzügigen Budget zu, um Ökologen in wissenschaftlichen Instrumenten des Landschaftsmanagements auszubilden.

Eine Zuteilung von Geldern durch das Parlament war ziemlich ungewöhnlich und führte unter den Biologen zu Spannungen, da Anträge eigentlich den Norwegischen Forschungsrat durchlaufen mussten. Der Botaniker Knut Fægri (1909–2001) beispielsweise beklagte, die Ökologie sei mittlerweile „eine schöne Welt, die in hübschen Berichten an das Parlament und andere Behörden von sich reden macht ... Aber haben sie [die Ökologen] eine Ahnung davon, was sie tun?".[29] Fægri war beunruhigt, dass derlei Beihilfen zu Lasten der Systematik gehen könnten, und fragte sich, ob die Ökologen ihre Versprechungen überhaupt würden einlösen können. Seine Sorgen waren nicht unbegründet, da die Systematik fortan in den Hintergrund rückte.

Als die Mitglieder des internationalen Biologischen Programms ihre wissenschaftlich Forschung aufnahmen, spielte die anfängliche Ausrichtung auf Managementinstrumente und Produktion eine weniger große Rolle. Hervorgehoben wurde stattdessen die Bedeutung der umweltnahen Erholung – ganz besonders in der personell stärksten Wissenschaftlergruppe, die in Finse arbeitete. Ofiziell nannte sich ihr Forschungsvorhaben „Erzeugnisse terrestrischer Gemeinschaften" und „Nutzung und Bewirtschaftung biologischer Ressourcen", wobei allerdings die meis-

on would take a backstage role.

When it came to the scientific research done by the International Biological Program scholars, the initial focus on managerial tools and production became less important. The importance of environmental recreation became instead the imperative, especially among the largest group of scholars working at Finse. The official title of their research project was "Production of Terrestrial Communities" and "Use and Management of Biological Resources", while most of them were critical to the utilitarian perspective these titles suggested. Vik stressed that ecologists were "working with and not against nature".[30] Similarly, Dahl saw a difference between "product science and environmental science", in which science that produces "products to live on" must be contrasted to research on "a good environment to live in" as places suitable for "recreation".[31] To him the difference between "to research on" and "to live in" the environment signified technocratic versus ecological ways of thinking. In their research ecologists would thus emphasize non-economic values. Typically, an intramural research report about reindeer would stress "the aesthetic importance of these animals to walkers in the area".[32] Such comments should be understood in the context of the culture of mountaineering and outdoor-life from which most ecologists emerged. As the professor of botany and Minister of Agriculture Olav Gjærevoll (1916–94) argued:

The increasing urbanization and heavy traffic creates a major need for areas in which humans can find rest, recreation, peace and nature experience. This will demand a significant adjustment in our entire way of thinking about area planning. Thriving-areas must be chosen after a quality evaluation of nature. In our legislation we must draw the conclusion that these thriving-areas must be protected. Any Norwegian must admit that our most important thriving-areas are the beaches and the mountains.[33]

Recreation was a way in which humans could be energized through outdoor life in the steady-state of nature's energy circulation. This was especially important to urban dwellers without direct contact with nature. To protect this possibility, recreation took the centre stage as an ecologically sound alternative to large-scale plans for hydro-power developments of water systems from high mountains deep down to the fjords. When such plans were proposed for a large mountain plateau, Hardangervidda near Finse, in 1968, for example, they were met with head-on resistance from ecologists who used these rivers to determine the steady-state of the plateau.[34] As ecology was defined as the study of relations one thus had to protect the entire area as an untouched reference environment: "Hardangervidda is one unit, and

ten Forscher die in diesen Titeln mitschwingende funktionellen Perspektive kritisierten. Ökologen, hob Vik hervor, „arbeiten mit der Natur und nicht gegen sie".[30] Ähnlich sah Dahl einen Unterschied zwischen „Produktwissenschaft und Umweltwissenschaft", weshalb man der Wissenschaft, die „Produkte" erzeuge, „von denen man lebt", die Forschung nach „einer guten Umwelt, in der man lebt" und die zur „Erholung" geeignet sei, entgegenstellen müsse.[31] Für ihn machte „Forschen über die" versus „Leben in der" Umwelt den Unterschied zwischen technokratischer und ökologischer Denkweise aus. Folglich betonten die Ökologen in ihrer Forschung nichtökonomische Werte. Bezeichnenderweise unterstrich ein interner Forschungsbericht über Rentiere „die ästhetische Bedeutung dieser Tiere für Wanderer in der Gegend".[32] Solche Kommentare sind im kulturellen Kontext des Bergsteigens und Freilandlebens zu verstehen, aus dem die meisten Ökologen hervorgegangen sind. So argumentierte der Professor für Botanik und Landwirtschaftsminister Olav Gjærevoll (1916–94):

„Aus der zunehmenden Verstädterung und dem hohen Verkehrsaufkommen ergibt sich ein gesteigertes Bedürfnis nach Räumen, in denen die Menschen Ruhe, Erholung und Frieden finden und Natur erleben können. Daher wird es erforderlich sein, unsere Raumplanungsauffassung insgesamt deutlich zu korrigieren. Geboten ist eine qualitative Evaluierung der Natur und entsprechende Auswahl von Naturentwicklungsräumen. Deren Schutz müssen wir in unserer Gesetzgebung festschreiben. Alle Norweger sollten anerkennen, dass unsere wichtigsten Naturentwicklungsräume die Strände und die Berge sind."[33]

Erholung konnte heißen, Menschen durch Freilandleben im Fließgleichgewicht des natürlichen Energiekreislaufs energetisch aufzuladen. Besonders wichtig war das für Städter ohne direkte Berührung zur Natur. Um diese Möglichkeit zu wahren, erhielt die Erholung eine Schlüsselstellung als ökologisch verträgliche Alternative zu Großprojekten für Wasserkraftwerke, deren Anlagen vom Hochgebirge bis tief hinab in die Fjords reichen sollten. Als etwa 1968 solche Pläne für das weitläufige Bergplateau Hardangervidda bei Finse vorgelegt wurden, stießen sie auf den frontalen Widerstand von Ökologen, die anhand der Wasserläufe das Fließgleichgewicht des Plateaus ermittelten.[34] Da Ökologie als Untersuchung der Beziehungen definiert war, galt es den Gesamtraum als unberührte Referenzumwelt zu schützen: „Hardangervidda ist eine Einheit und sollte als eine Einheit erhalten bleiben", argumentierten sie.[35] Örtliche Planer zogen diese Forscher im Mai 1969 als wissenschaftliche Sachverständige heran und inaugurierten damit einen Verfahrensweg, auf dem die Ökologen bei Zukunftsentwicklungen ein Mitspracherecht hatten. Für Vik stellte dies „ein neues Kapitel in der Geschichte" der Umweltdebatte dar.[36] Ökologie als

should thus be preserved as one unit", they argued.[35] In May 1969 local planners called them in as scientific experts, and established with this a procedure in which ecologists would have a say in future developments. To Vik this represented "a new chapter in the history" of environmental debate.[36] Ecology as applied science with ecologists as activist scholars and counter expertise to engineers also caught the attention of young environmentalist philosophers who saw them as allies in their fight against the "technocratic politics" they associated with positivist philosophy.[37] In the end, most of the hydro-power plans for Hardangervidda were either scaled down or abandoned and the plateau was instead designated for ecological research and vacationing. The success gave, as one ecologist pointed out, "aim and meaning in life" in a secularized world.[38]

One of the Finse ecologists fighting hydro-power developments was the zoologist Ivar Mysterud (b. 1938). He was also in the midst of the environmental debate at the University of Oslo, and instrumental in giving it an ecological perspective. He worked next-door to Kvaløy, whom he engaged, along with Næss, in numerous discussions. It was through these conversations that many of the Oslo philosophers and other non-biologists learned about ecological concepts and terms. He also wrote several introductory articles that were widely read among students of ecology, environmentalists, and philosophers at the university. Most important, perhaps, were his lectures and seminars in which he and a series of his colleagues explained in non-technical terms the nature of ecology and pollution to a broad audience. Though not best-sellers, his publications became standard references and would frame debates about pollution in terms of steady-state and ecological energy circulation for at least a decade.[39]

Despite all the efforts, Mysterud felt in 1969 that there was not enough time to understand the ecosystems, before the industrial society – like a "cancer abscess"– would destroy them.[40] 1970 was the European Year for Conservation of Nature which, according to Mysterud, developed into a "national championship in oral environmentalism". Frustrated by lack of action, he decided, with Magnar Norderhaug (1939–2006), to turn the talking "towards deeper social issues" such as the questioning of economic growth.[41] Politics should be put on a secure ecological footing, they argued, and suggested the term 'eco-politics' to distance phoney environmentalism from the real thing. The term was quickly adopted not only by fellow ecologists, but also by a series of scholars, activists, and students questioning technocracy and industrialism. Much of this criticism had since the mid-1960s been informed by populist agrarian socialism, which, thanks to Mysterud and

angewandte Wissenschaft mit Ökologen als aktivistischen Wissenschaftlern, die Gutachten gegen Ingenieure erstellten – das erweckte auch die Aufmerksamkeit junger Umweltphilosophen, die hier Verbündete in ihrem Kampf gegen die „technokratische Politik" erkannten, die sie mit der positivistischen Philosophie in Zusammenhang brachten.[37] Am Ende wurden die meisten Wasserkraftpläne für Hardangervidda entweder verkleinert oder aufgegeben; stattdessen wurde das Plateau als Forschungs- und Urlaubsgebiet ausgewiesen. Dieser Erfolg gab, wie ein Ökologe hervorhob, „dem Leben Ziel und Bedeutung" in einer säkularisierten Welt.[38]

Einer der Ökologen, die in Finse gegen die Wasserkrafterschließungen kämpften, war der Zoologe Ivar Mysterud (geb. 1938). Er stand auch im Zentrum der Umweltdebatte an der Universität Oslo und wirkte entscheidend daran mit, ihr eine ökologische Perspektive zu verleihen. Er arbeitete Tür an Tür mit Kvaløy, den er, nebst Næss, in etliche Diskussionen verwickelte. Durch diese Gespräche erfuhren viele Osloer Philosophen und andere Nicht-Biologen von ökologischen Konzepten und Begriffen. Mysterud schrieb auch einige unter Studenten der Ökologie, Umweltschützern und Philosophen an der Universität viel gelesene Einführungstexte. Am bedeutsamsten waren vielleicht seine Vorlesungen und Seminare, in denen er und einige seiner Kollegen einem breiten Publikum Ökologie und Umweltverschmutzung allgemein verständlich erklärten. Seine Veröffentlichungen waren zwar keine Bestseller, wurden aber zu Standardwerken und konturierten mindestens ein Jahrzehnt lang die Debatten über die Folgen der Umweltverschmutzung für das Fließgleichgewicht und den ökologischen Energiekreislauf.[39]

Trotz aller Bemühungen erkannte Mysterud 1969, dass die Zeit zu knapp war, um die Ökosysteme zu verstehen, bevor die Industriegesellschaft sie – wie ein „Krebsgeschwür" – zerstören würde.[40] 1970 war das Europäische Naturschutzjahr, das sich laut Mysterud zu einer „Nationalmeisterschaft in verbalem Umweltbewusstsein" entwickelte. Frustriert von der Tatenlosigkeit beschloss er zusammen mit Magnar Norderhaug (1939–2006), „tiefere soziale Fragen" wie etwa die Zweifelhaftigkeit des Wirtschaftswachstums zur Sprache zu bringen.[41] Die Politik sollte auf sichere ökologische Füße gestellt werden, meinten die beiden, und schlugen das Wort „Ökopolitik" vor, um bloße Umwelttümelei von echtem Engagement abzutrennen. Rasch wurde der Begriff nicht nur von Kollegen übernommen, sondern auch von einigen Wissenschaftlern, Aktivisten und Studenten, die Technokratie und Industrialismus hinterfragten. Viel von dieser Kritik war seit Mitte der 1960er Jahre geprägt durch den populistischen Agrarsozialismus, der dank Mysterud und Norderhaug von 1970 an unter dem neuen Label Ökopolitik weitermachte.[42] Anders als die Sozialisten suchten Mysterud und

Norderhaug, continued under the new label of eco-politics from 1970 and onwards.[42] Unlike the socialists, however, Mysterud and Norderhaug sought an eco-politics founded on science, as our common future depended on a developing a "steady-state" social economy mirroring the steady-state balance of the economy of nature they knew from Finse.[43] They saw no technical solutions to the eco-crisis, as this depended on uncontrollable economic growth. Instead they searched for an alternative technology in tune with ecological principles of zero-growth and steady-state.[44]

One of many students inspired by their steady-state reasoning was the young graduate Nils Christian Stenseth (b. 1949), who later became a key figure in international ecological research. His first article, published when he was twenty-three years old, was about eco-politics. "Based on their knowledge", he argued, "all biologists should work for st*eady state society to* replace growth society", and one should limit the human population growth to zero.[45] Ecological modelling represented to Stenseth the way forward, as simulation models could determine the exact nature of when and how to achieve a steady-state. He was well aware of the practical and theoretical problems in construing such a representation of the world, and therefore devoted his Ph.D. to the topic. He was not alone, as computer modelling was "about to become an independent ecological branch of research" in this period.[46]

Student environmentalists and the ecophilosophy group

At the University, many were impressed with the ecologists' scientific backing of their environmental concerns. They had, as Næss put it, a "tremendous and almost sinister responsibility for our society's future".[47] This approval was especially apparent among students who, thanks to the ecologists, would transform their aesthetic appreciation of scenic nature into broader concerns for environments as a whole.

One event that became important in triggering a call to action among the environmentally concerned at the University was the exhibition, *And after us …*, created by students of the Oslo School of Architecture in June 1969. They drew attention to the possibility of children "after us" having no environment to live in.[48] It was a travelling exhibition of ecological doom and gloom seen by eighty thousand people in Oslo alone, inspired by Vik's popular writings about the eco-crisis and sponsored by the Norwegian Society for the Conservation of Nature.[49] With the help of dramatic graphic design, the architects crystallized a clear message about its being either a disaster or a harmonious balanced ecosystem "after us". This either/or dichotomy between a future of industrial

Nordhaug jedoch nach einer wissenschaftlich fundierten Ökopolitik, da die gemeinsame Zukunft davon abhing, eine Sozialökonomie des „Fließgleichgewichts" zu entwickeln, die das ihnen aus Finse bekannte Fließgleichgewicht der Naturökonomie widerspiegeln sollte.[43] Ihnen zufolge gab es für die Ökokrise keine technischen Lösungen, da diese auf unkontrollierbares Wirtschaftswachstum angewiesen seien. Stattdessen suchten sie nach einer auf die ökologischen Grundsätze des Nullwachstums und des Fließgleichgewichts abgestimmten Alternativtechnologie.[44]

Einer von vielen durch ihr Fließgleichgewichts-Denken angeregten Studenten war der junge Hochschulabsolvent Nils Christian Stenseth (geb. 1949), der später zu einer Schlüsselfigur in der internationalen ökologischen Forschung avancierte. Sein erster Artikel, den er als 23-Jähriger publizierte, handelte von Ökopolitik. „Auf ihre Erkenntnissen aufbauend", legte er dar, „sollten sich alle Biologen für eine Gesellschaft des Fließgleichgewichts einsetzen, die anstelle der Wachstumsgesellschaft tritt", außerdem solle man das Wachstum der Weltbevölkerung auf Null begrenzen.[45] Ökologische Modellbildung wies für Stenseth den Weg nach vorn, da Simulationsmodelle exakt bestimmen könnten, wann und wie ein Fließgleichgewicht erreicht werde. Er war sich der praktischen und theoretischen Probleme bei der Konstruktion einer solchen Weltdarstellung durchaus bewusst und widmete deshalb diesem Thema seine Promotionsarbeit. Dabei war er nicht der einzige, denn Computermodellierung „entwickelte sich" in dieser Zeit „zu einem eigenständigen ökologischen Forschungszweig".[46]

Studentische Umweltschützer und die Ökophilosophische Gruppe

An der Universität war man vielfach beeindruckt von der wissenschaftlichen Rückendeckung für die eigenen Umweltsorgen. Denn man sah sich ja, wie Næss es ausdrückte, in einer „gewaltigen, ja nahezu ungeheuren Verantwortung für die Zukunft unserer Gesellschaft".[47] Zuspruch kam zumal aus der Studentenschaft, die dank der Ökologen von der ästhetischen Wertschätzung für eine malerische Natur zu einem gesamtheitlichen Umweltbewusstsein fand.

Ein Ereignis wirkte in der universitären Umweltbewegung in besonderem Maße als Aufruf zum Handeln: die Wanderausstellung *Und nach uns*, die im Juni 1969 von Studenten der Architekturhochschule Oslo ausgerichtet wurde und darauf aufmerksam machte, dass die Kinder „nach uns" möglicherweise keine Lebensumwelt mehr haben würden.[48] Die düstere Wanderausstellung über den ökologischen Untergang, die von Viks viel gelesenen Texten über die Ökokrise angeregt war und Fördergelder vom Norwegischen Naturschutzbund bekam, wurde allein in Oslo von 8000 Besuchern gesehen.[49] Mithilfe einer

doom or ecological bliss came to dominate the environmental debate in Norway, thanks to the emerging group of ecophilosophers.

Kvaløy was greatly impressed by the exhibition, and invited the architects to join hands with students of ecology, philosophers, and technical climbers from the Alpine Club, to create a Co-working Group for the Protection of Nature and the Environment at the University. Those with a philosophical bent met in the Ecophilosophy Group, a subsection of this loose association. These students were largely from the Department of Philosophy, which was at the time in turmoil after a week-long student occupation of the department in January 1969 led by radicals and followers of Mao. They demanded a new curriculum, which in effect meant abandoning a syllabus arranged by Næss. He was then fifty-seven years old, and very much represented the old guard. His philosophies, developed in wake of his visit to the Vienna Circle in the early 1930s, were not an asset to students who thought of positivism as another word for the administrative nihilism they associated with the technocratic military complex and the Vietnam War.[50] As a consequence of students' demand for larger control, Næss left his seminar *Nature and Humans* in the hands of the students and departed to his cottage. In his office he left Kvaløy in charge with "a pile of the Department's letter-paper with Arne's signatures – in the middle, further down, and at the bottom", so that he could expedite things as he thought best.[51] This enabled Kvaløy to organize the *Nature and Humans* seminar according to his own mind, and the Ecophilosophy Group would thus occupy Næss's seminar from the autumn of 1969 through the spring semester of 1970, after which they would meet at the Department of Zoology where Mysterud worked.[52]

Though the ecophilosophers were to have an equal say, Kvaløy would actually set the agenda of the seminar. His mountaineering interests from the Alpine Club would initially provide the context, although the debate would gradually shift towards ecological concerns about the harmony of nature as this was expressed by Mysterud and other ecologists. What started with reflections about the recreational quality of mountains and waterfalls would thus lead to social criticism concerning industrialism's lack of steady-state and ecologically informed thinking about the human status within the environment's energy flux. It was not a shift without tensions. The historian of science Nils Roll-Hansen, for example, accused the ecophilosophers of favouring an "escape from the daily reality to the vacation paradise" of untouched nature.[53] In the end broader eco-political ideas for a steady-state society came to dominate, after two years of debating everything from ecology

dramatischen Szenografie formulierten die Architekten die unmissverständliche Botschaft, „nach uns" werde es entweder eine Katastrophe geben oder ein harmonisch ausgewogenes Ökosystem. Diese Entweder-Oder-Dichotomie zwischen einer Zukunft industriellen Untergangs oder ökologischen Segens gab dank der sich formierenden Gruppe der Ökophilosophen in Norwegen schließlich den Ton an.

Kvaløy war von der Ausstellung sehr beeindruckt und lud die Architekten dazu ein, sich mit Studenten der Ökologie, Philosophen und versierten Bergsteigern aus dem Alpenverein zusammenzutun, um an der Universität eine Coworking-Gruppe für Naturschutz und Umwelt zu gründen. Philosophisch Interessierte trafen sich in der Ökophilosophischen Gruppe, einer Untersektion dieses losen Verbunds. Meistens kamen sie aus der Philosophischen Abteilung, die sich seinerzeit im Aufruhr befand, nachdem Studenten sie im Januar 1969 unter der Führung von Radikalen und Maoisten eine Woche lang besetzt hatten. Sie forderten ein neues Curriculum, was darauf hinauslief, einen von Næss ausgearbeiteten Lehrplan fallen zu lassen. Næss war damals 57 Jahre alt und stand weitgehend für die alte Garde. Seine philosophischen Anschauungen, die einem Besuch des Wiener Kreises in den frühen 1930er Jahren entflossen, waren keine Bereicherung für Studenten, denen der Positivismus als Synonym für den administrativen Nihilismus galt, den sie mit dem technokratischen militärischen Komplex und dem Vietnamkrieg in Verbindung brachten.[50] Infolge des studentischen Anspruchs auf mehr Selbstverwaltung übergab Næss sein Seminar *Natur und Menschen* der Verantwortung der Studenten und zog sich in seine Kate zurück. Zur freien Verfügung Kvaløys hinterließ er in seinem Büro „einen Stapel Briefpapier der Abteilung mit Arnes Unterschriften – in der Mitte, etwas weiter unten und ganz am Ende", so dass dieser die Sache nach eigenem Gutdünken vorantreiben konnte.[51] Damit war Kvaløy imstande, das Seminar *Natur und Menschen* in seinem Sinn zu organisieren, so dass die Ökophilosophische Gruppe Næss' Seminar vom Herbst 1969 bis zum Frühjahrssemester 1970 okkupierte, wonach sie sich in der Abteilung für Zoologie traf, in der Mysterud arbeitete.[52]

Obwohl die Ökophilosophen gleiches Mitspracherecht hatten, bestimmte im Grunde Kvaløy das Programm des Seminars. Anfangs gaben seine aus dem Alpenverein rührenden Interessen für die Bergsteigerei den Kontext vor, doch verschob die Debatte sich schrittweise zu ökologischen Fragen der Naturharmonie, wie Mysterud und andere Ökologen sie formulierten. Was als Überlegungen über den Erholungswert von Bergen und Wasserfällen begann, führte demnach zu einer Sozialkritik am fehlenden Fließgleichgewicht des Industrialismus und zu einem ökologisch geprägten Denken über die Stellung des Menschen im Energiefluss der Umwelt. Diese Ver-

to topics such as the psychology of perception, social psychology and anthropology, nature philosophy, pedagogy, information theory, thermodynamics, and cybernetics.

The ecophilosophers and the Co-working Group had a significant effect on students seeking radicalism within acceptable socio-political boundaries of the Cold War. They were neither leftist nor rightist and thus non-threatening in the bipolar political terrain. "What we stand for may seem archconservative and at the same time extremely radical", Kvaløy argued. "We will therefore strike in both directions, and we will be attacked from all sides."[54] They became an effective hard-hitting student association attacking hydro-power developments in particular. Most dramatic was their attempt to save the Mardøla River, which included Norway's highest waterfall, during the summer vacation of 1970. The demonstration evolved into a dramatic civil disobedience sit-in with more than one hundred and fifty protesters blocking the construction site, followed by fifty journalists covering the story. In the end the demonstrators left voluntarily or, as in the case of Kvaløy and Næss, were carried away by the police. Though they had some support from the neighbourhood farmers, they had no sympathy from local workers who saw nature as a resource securing their jobs. They threatened them with beating and banners such as: "HIPPIES GO HOME – IF YOU HAVE ONE" and "TRY SOMETHING NEW – WHAT ABOUT A JOB?"[55] In fact most of the demonstrators had jobs, many of them at the University of Oslo. The underlying issue at stake was instead how to understand nature. Was it a resource securing jobs, a scenic place in which to enjoy country-life vacations, or an environment in which humans should learn to live in a steady-state?

Næss was brought to Mardøla in the last dramatic week of the demonstration, so that the media could get an image of the famous philosopher being taken away by the police. This sense of being involved with the young was important to Næss, given the occupation of the Department of Philosophy only a year earlier. Indeed, he decided to liberate himself from all professorial duties and resigned his professorship at the end of 1970, so that he could devote himself fully to the environmental cause, and thereby refashion himself as a philosopher of current affairs. His students were quoting Karl Marx: "The philosophers have only interpreted the world in various ways; the point however is to change it."[56] Provoked by such statements, Næss decided to modify his thinking towards a more ideological stand in order to appeal to the young: "when we believe that we really must do something about some terrible pressing problem, we must somehow narrow down our perspective.... [Students] need rhetoric and dogmatism, I think.

lagerung ging nicht ohne Spannungen ab. Der Wissenschaftshistoriker Nils Roll-Hansen zum Beispiel warf den Ökophilosophen vor, sie begünstigten eine „Flucht aus der täglichen Realität in das Urlaubsparadies" unberührter Natur.[53] Am Ende gewannen umfassendere ökopolitische Ideen hinsichtlich einer Gesellschaft des Fließgleichgewichts die Oberhand, nachdem man zwei Jahre über alles mögliche diskutiert hatte, von der Ökologie bis zu Themen wie Wahrnehmungspsychologie, Sozialpsychologie und Anthropologie, Naturphilosophie, Pädagogik, Informationstheorie, Thermodynamik und Kybernetik.

Die Ökophilosophen und die Coworking-Gruppe zogen in erheblichem Umfang Studenten an, die nach einer radikalen Position innerhalb der akzeptablen soziopolitischen Grenzen des Kalten Krieges suchten. Es waren dies weder Linke noch Rechte, weshalb sie auf dem bipolaren politischen Terrain keine Bedrohung darstellten. „Wofür wir stehen, mag erzkonservativ und gleichzeitig extrem radikal erscheinen", erklärte Kvaløy. „Deshalb werden wir in beiden Richtungen zustoßen, und man wird uns von allen Seiten angreifen."[54] Daraus entstand eine schlagkräftige Studentenvereinigung, die in erster Linie gegen Wasserkrafterschließungen vorging. Besonders aufsehenerregend war ihr in den Sommerferien 1970 unternommener Versuch, den Fluss Mardøla zu retten, in dem sich Norwegens höchster Wasserfall befindet. Die Demonstration mündete in ein dramatisches Sit-in, bei dem 150 Protestierende in zivilem Ungehorsam die Baustelle blockierten, gefolgt von 50 Journalisten, die darüber berichteten. Am Ende räumten die Demonstranten freiwillig das Gelände oder wurden, wie Kvaløy und Næss, von der Polizei weggetragen. Eine gewisse Unterstützung kam aus der benachbarten Bauernschaft, keinerlei Sympathie aber von den örtlichen Arbeitern, die in der Natur eine arbeitsplatzsichernde Ressource sahen. Sie drohten den Demonstranten Prügel an und schwenkten Transparente wie „HIPPIES GEHT NACH HAUSE – WENN IHR EINS HABT" und „VERSUCHT MAL WAS NEUES – WIE WÄR'S MIT EINER ARBEIT?".[55] Dabei waren die meisten Demonstranten durchaus berufstätig, viele von ihnen an der Universität Oslo. Das Grundproblem lag vielmehr im Verständnis der Natur. War sie eine Ressource, um Arbeitsplätze zu sichern, ein reizvolles Gebiet, um Ferien auf dem Land zu genießen, oder eine Umwelt, in der die Menschen lernen sollten, im Fließgleichgewicht zu leben?

Während der dramatischen letzten Woche der Demonstration wurde Næss zum Mardøla gebracht, so dass die Medien bildmächtig festhalten konnten, wie der berühmte Philosoph von der Polizei weggetragen wurde. Angesichts der Besetzung der Abteilung für Philosophie vor gerade einmal einem Jahr war es Næss ein Anliegen, sich mit den jungen Leuten zusammenzutun. Dementsprechend beschloss er,

[Philosophical] Scepticism breeds passivity. I do not feel that way, but the students do."[57]

The students he is referring to were those in Ecophilosophy Group, as he would attend their meetings from the autumn of 1970. According to Mysterud, he was one of the few who took notes, and in the spring of 1971 he would transform them into a couple of lectures entitled *Ecology and Philosophy*. In them he introduced, for the first time, his ecosophy ... as a type of philosophy that takes its point of departure in an identification with all life, in this life-giving environment. It establishes in a way a classless society within the entire biosphere, a democracy in which we can talk about a justice not only for humans, but also for animals, plants, and minerals. And life will not be conceived as an antagonism to death, but in interaction with surroundings, the life-giving environment. This represents a very strong emphasis on everything hanging together and that we are only *fragments* – not even parts.[58]

The eco-centric notion of humans as fragments of a larger whole was inspired not only by the ecological view of species as fragments in nature's energy-circulation, but also by Chinese social philosophy. The politics of Mao was in vogue among those young philosophers who had occupied Næss's former department, and his collected poems had just been translated into Norwegian. They include a rich body of metaphors concerning nature's harmony, which caught Næss's attention. Thus he would claim that in China "the human being is not in the foreground, but instead an entire 'ecological system', in which humans take part as fragments. Mao has perhaps kept a part of the classical Chinese outlook. In his political poetry animals, plants, minerals, and landscape elements have a place that seems ludicrous to rough Western observers".[59] The harmony of nature Mao endorsed, it is worth noting, was rough to both nature and humans, treating them indeed as fragments. Yet Næss would, like many of his contemporaries, fail to see this. Eager to gain acceptance, he wrote a sympathetic booklet about Mao, and included Mao's thinking in a revised edition of his history of philosophy textbook in which he went out of his way to appeal to young radicals, as it was required reading for *all* the students at the University. The book had, for a while, a portrait of Mao on its front cover.[60]

The Mardøla experience and the discussions at the Institute of Biology about ecological steady-state would also energize and radicalize students within the Ecophilosophy Group. This was especially the case in the thinking of Kvaløy, their unofficial charismatic leader. After the Mardøla experience, he adapted the idea from ecology that a complex ecosystem is more robust than a simple one in the

sich von allen Professorenpflichten zu befreien und legte Ende 1970 sein akademisches Amt nieder, damit er sich ganz der Sache der Umwelt widmen und in diesem Zuge zu einem Philosophen für laufende Angelegenheiten umdefinieren konnte. Seine Studenten zitierten Karl Marx: „Die Philosophen haben die Welt nur verschieden interpretiert, es kommt aber darauf an, sie zu verändern."[56] Von solchen Aussagen herausgefordert, beschloss Næss, sein Denken stärker ideologisch auszurichten, um die Jugend zu erreichen: „Wenn wir glauben, dass wir an einem schrecklich drängenden Problem etwas tun müssen, müssen wir in gewisser Weise unsere Perspektive enger führen … [Studenten] brauchen Rhetorik und dogmatische Vorgaben, glaube ich. [Philosophischer] Skeptizismus erzeugt Passivität. Ich selbst empfinde zwar nicht so, wohl aber die Studenten."[57]

Damit bezog er sich auf die Studenten der Ökophilosophischen Gruppe, deren Versammlungen er seit Herbst 1970 besuchte. Als einer der wenigen schrieb er mit, wie Mysterud sich erinnert, und verarbeitete seine Aufzeichnungen im Frühjahr 1971 zu einer Vorlesungsreihe mit dem Titel *Ökologie und Philosophie*. Dort sprach er erstmals von seiner „Ökosophie … als einer Ausprägung der Philosophie, die ihren Ausgangspunkt in einer Identifikation mit jedwedem Leben in der lebensspendenden Umwelt nimmt. Sie etabliert gewissermaßen eine klassenlose Gesellschaft in der Biosphäre, eine Demokratie, in der wir von Gerechtigkeit nicht nur für Menschen, sondern auch für Tiere, Pflanzen und Mineralien reden können. Dabei wird das Leben nicht als Antagonismus zum Tod, sondern in seinem Zusammenspiel mit der Umgebung, der lebensspendenden Umwelt aufgefasst. Hierdurch ist nachdrücklich betont, dass alles zusammenhängt und wir nur Fragmente – nicht einmal Teile – sind."[58]

Das ökozentrische Verständnis von den Menschen als Fragmenten eines größeren Ganzen griff nicht nur zurück auf die ökologische Auffassung von den Arten als Fragmenten im Energiekreislauf der Natur, sondern auch auf die chinesische Sozialphilosophie. Maos Politik war angesagt bei den jungen Philosophen, die Næess' Abteilung besetzt hatten, und die gesammelten Gedichte des Großen Vorsitzenden waren soeben ins Norwegische übertragen worden. Sie enthalten einen reichen Metaphernschatz zur Harmonie der Natur, auf den Næss aufmerksam wurde. So erklärte er, in China stehe „nicht der Mensch im Vordergrund, sondern vielmehr das gesamte ‚ökologische System', in dem Menschen als Fragmente einbeschlossen sind. Mao hat möglicherweise einen Teil der klassischen chinesischen Sichtweise beibehalten. In seiner politischen Poesie kommt Tieren, Pflanzen, Mineralien und Landschaftselementen eine Stellung zu, die grobianischen westlichen Beobachtern grotesk erscheint".[59] Die Naturharmonie, für die Mao eintrat, war bemerkenswerterweise grobianisch

face of environmental changes. Inspired by Herbert Marcuse, he argued that a complex human society would have a better chance of surviving the environmental crisis than the "one dimensional man" of the industrial society.[61] What living in an ecological steady-state society entailed was initially rather unclear, though it implied some sort of agrarian "green lung" away from industrial and urban pollution.[62] A comprehensive "eco-philosophy" addressing these issues, Kvaløy noted in his orientation to the Group in May 1971, "has not yet been formulated". It was still at "the sketching stage".[63] It was not until after Kvaløy's subsequent vacation in Nepal that he came to formulate a clear alternative to Western industrialism.

Oriental vacationing and the critique of the west

What made the Norwegian history of ecology somewhat different was the way in which ecophilosophers came to construe nature as an Oriental harmony juxtaposed against harsh Occidental values of Western capitalism.[64] This demarcation between Oriental ecological wisdom and the Occidental stupidity of the West was made possible through a series of vacations to Pakistan, India and Nepal by Næss, Faarlund and Kvaløy. It was this eco-tourism that eventually came to frame the deep-ecological debate at home and abroad.

One of Næss's most pleasurable climbing memories was his vacation to the northwest tribal region of Pakistan in 1950. It was organized as an "expedition" by the Alpine Club so that its members could climb the mountain Tirich Mir and provide friends at home with thrilling accounts of how they, after much struggle, managed to plant a Norwegian flag on the top of the mountain. The Norwegian Geographical Society added a scientific aspect to the journey by sponsoring the twenty-two-year-old student Per Wendelbo (1927–81), who later published a study of the region's flora.[65] Judging from the travel accounts, however, climbing was the all-dominating focus, along with playing polo matches organized by local officials who went out their way to entertain the Norwegian tourists. In 1964 they repeated the success with another climbing vacation to Tirich Mir. Næss would explain his thriving as a technical climber as a mixture of pain and excitement in mathematical terms as $T = G^2/(L_s + Å_s)$. Here T "trivsel" ("thriving") equalled G^2 "gløv" ("excitement") divided by L_s "legemlige smerter" ("bodily pains") plus $Å_s$ "åndelige smerter" ("spiritual pains"). This formula would later re-emerge as a key explanation of the meaning of self-realization in Næss's "Ecosophy T", with the 'T' being short for "thriving".[66]

Equally important to his ecosophy was Mahatma Gandhi's teaching of nonviolence, who came to the

sowohl zur Natur als auch zu den Menschen, die in der Tat als Fragmente behandelt wurden. Dies aber hat Næss wie viele seiner Zeitgenossen verkannt. Um Anerkennung bemüht, verfasste er über Mao eine verständnisinnige Broschüre und nahm Maos Denken in eine überarbeitete Ausgabe seiner Textsammlung zur Philosophiegeschichte auf, in der er keine Mühen scheute, junge Radikale anzusprechen, da das Buch für alle Studenten an der Universität Pflichtlektüre war. Das Frontcover zeigte eine Zeitlang ein Mao-Porträt.[60]

Die Mardøla-Erfahrung und die Diskussionen über das ökologische Fließgleichgewicht, die im Institut für Biologie stattfanden, sollten auch Studenten der Ökophilosophischen Gruppe befeuern und radikalisieren. Besonders galt dies für Kvaløy, ihren charismatischen inoffiziellen Anführer. Nach der Mardøla-Erfahrung machte er sich aus der Ökologie den Gedanken zueigen, dass ein komplexes Ökosystem gegenüber Umweltveränderungen widerstandsfähiger ist als ein einfaches. Angeregt durch Herbert Marcuse argumentierte er, eine komplexe menschliche Gesellschaft werde bessere Aussichten haben, die Umweltkrise zu überleben, als der „eindimensionale Mensch" der Industriegesellschaft.[61] Was das Leben in einer Gesellschaft des ökologischen Fließgleichgewichts bedeutete, war anfänglich recht unklar, jedenfalls aber implizierte es eine Art agrarische „grüne Lunge" abseits industrieller und urbaner Umweltverschmutzung.[62] Eine systematische „Ökophilosophie" in diesen Belangen, hielt Kvaløy im Mai 1971 in seiner Einführung für die Gruppe fest, „ist noch nicht ausgearbeitet". Sie sei noch im „Entwurfsstadium".[63] Erst nach seinem anschließenden Urlaub in Nepal konnte Kvaløy eine klare Alternative zum westlichen Industrialismus formulieren.

Urlaub im fernen Osten und die Kritik am Westen

Die norwegische Geschichte der Ökologie verlief insofern ein wenig anders, als die dortigen Ökophilosophen die Natur als östliche Harmonie zu deuten lernten, die sie den rauen Werten des westlichen Kapitalismus entgegensetzten.[64] Möglich wurde die Abgrenzung zwischen morgenländischer ökologischer Weisheit und abendländischer Dummheit des Westens durch eine Reihe von Urlaubsreisen, die Næss, Faarlund und Kvaløy nach Pakistan, Indien und Nepal führten. Dieser Ökotourismus war es, der letztlich die tiefenökologische Debatte im In- und Ausland konturierte.

Zu Næss' schönsten Erinnerungen als Bergsteiger zählte der Urlaub, den er 1950 in Pakistans nordwestlichem Stammesgebiet verbrachte. Dieser wurde vom Alpenverein als „Expedition" organisiert, damit die Mitglieder den Berg Tirich Mir erstbesteigen und die Freunde in der Heimat mit spannenden Berichten darüber versorgen konnten, wie sie nach vielen Anstrengungen schließlich die norwegische Fahne auf

forefront of Næss's thinking after his first visit to Pakistan in 1950. Back in Oslo he gave a lecture series about Gandhi's political ethics which resulted in a book co-authored with the young sociologist Johan Galtung (b. 1930) and published in 1955.[67] Gandhi's teachings, they argued, could be helpful in finding a peaceful transition away from the Cold War deadlock. In 1960 Næss followed this up with a popular version, which was translated in 1965 as *Gandhi and the Nuclear Age*. Here he argued that people from the West had much to learn from Gandhi, given the threat of nuclear Armageddon. The book became Næss's first international success with favourable reviews in academic as well as popular journals. This was much welcome, as his previously published books and articles were generally ill-received or ignored.[68] What was especially encouraging with *Gandhi and the Nuclear Age* was its appeal to young students.

His young admirers, besides Galtung, included Kvaløy. They were loyal to their teacher, and in the spring of 1969 – in an attempt to heal the wounds of the students' occupation of the Philosophy Department – they took him on an eighteen-day road trip from Oslo to Varanasi in India where Næss was to spend a month peaceresearching. To judge from Kvaløy's charming flashback, the trip undoubtedly created some of his very fondest memories.[69] From Varanasi they went on a vacation to Nepal, where they climbed the top of the mountain Nagarkot north of Katmandu, before returning home to organize the Co-working Group for the Protection of Nature and the Environment and the Ecophilosophy Group. Kvaløy would return to India in the winter of 1969, and on his way home he climbed the Mount Damavand in Iran together with Stein Jarving (b. 1945), who, taken with Kvaløy's thinking, went home to found an ecological inspired steady-state farming community.[70]

After two years of environmental activism at home, Næss and Kvaløy returned to Nepal during the summer vacation of 1971, this time with their fellow-climber Faarlund. The journey was to be a two-month-long "pilgrimage" to the remote village of Beding in the Rolwaling valley of Nepal, and a vacation from the "garish, narcotic nightmare" of the European "consumer society".[71] They were following a larger trend of people searching Oriental wisdom and alternatives. In the early 1970s thousands of Western hippies went to Katmandu where they had their own "Freak Street" by Durbar Square in which they nurtured unconventional lifestyles and imagined Nepalese ways of living.[72]

The ecophilosophers' financial backing was less exotic, as the journey was paid for by Næss's half-brother, Erling (1901–93), who had become enor-

dem Berggipfel pflanzten. Einen wissenschaftlichen Beitrag zu der Exkursion leistete die Norwegische Geografische Gesellschaft in Form von Fördergeldern für den 22-jährigen Studenten Per Wendelbo (1927–81), der später eine Studie über die Flora der Region veröffentlichte.[65] Nach den Reiseberichten zu urteilen stand jedoch das Klettern ganz im Mittelpunkt, neben einigen Polopartien, organisiert von lokalen Amtsträgern, die keine Mühen scheuten, die norwegischen Touristen zu unterhalten. 1964 wiederholten diese ihren Erfolg mit einer weiteren Klettertour auf dem Tirich Mir. Næss erklärte seine Erfüllung als technischer Bergsteiger mit einer Mischung aus Schmerz und Beglückung, die er in die mathematische Formel $T = G^2/(L_S + Å_S)$ packte. T „trivsel" („Erfüllung") gleich G^2 „glød" („Beglückung") geteilt durch L_S „legemlige smerter" („körperliche Schmerzen") plus $Å_S$ „åndelige smerter" („geistig-seelische Schmerzen"). Mit dieser Formel erläuterte Næss später in seiner „Ökosophie T" die Kernbedeutung von Selbstverwirklichung, wobei „T" als Kürzel für „trivsel" steht.[66]

Ebenso maßgeblich für Næss' Ökosophie war Mahatma Gandhis Lehre der Gewaltlosigkeit, die nach dem ersten Pakistanbesuch im Jahr 1950 in den Vordergrund seines Denkens rückte. Zurück in Oslo hielt er eine Reihe von Vorträgen über Gandhis politische Ethik, die in einem gemeinsam mit dem jungen Soziologen Johan Galtung (geb. 1930) verfassten und 1955 publizierten Buch mündete.[67] Die beiden legten dar, Gandhis Lehren könnten dabei helfen, einen friedlichen Ausweg aus der Sackgasse des Kalten Krieges zu finden. 1960 ließ Næss dem Buch eine populärwissenschaftliche Version folgen, die 1965 unter dem Titel *Gandhi and the Nuclear Age* übersetzt wurde. Darin erklärte er, die Menschen des Westens hätten angesichts der Bedrohung durch eine globale nukleare Katastrophe viel von Gandhi zu lernen. Das Buch war Næss' erster internationaler Erfolg und wurde in akademischen wie auch in Publikumszeitschriften rezensiert. Dies war hoch willkommen, da seine zuvor veröffentlichten Bücher und Artikel meist schlecht aufgenommen oder ignoriert worden waren.[68] Besonders ermutigend war der Anklang, den *Gandhi and the Nuclear Age* bei jungen Studenten fand.

Neben Galtung zählte auch Kvaløy zu seinen jungen Bewunderern. Beide waren ihrem Lehrer treu verbunden und nahmen ihn im Frühjahr 1969 in einem Versuch, die von der studentischen Besetzung der Philosophischen Abteilung geschlagenen Wunden zu heilen, auf eine 18-tägige Autofahrt von Oslo nach Varanasi in Indien mit, wo Næss einen Monat lang Friedensforschung betreiben sollte. Nach Kvaløys anrührendem Rückblick zu urteilen, verschaffte ihm diese Reise eine seiner fraglos liebsten Erinnerungen.[69] Von Varanasi aus traten die drei einen Urlaub in Nepal an, wo sie zur östlich von Kathmandu in

mously wealthy through industrial whaling in the 1930s and shipping of oil in the 1960s. He took the ecophilosophers along to prove his cultural sincerity for Nepal to Prince Cayandendra and Maharaja Mayurbhany, whose personal financial interest he secured by establishing the state-sponsored Royal Nepal Shipping. Out of courtesy, the prince and the maharaja gave the necessary travel permissions to the ecophilosophers so that they could visit the closed-to-tourists village of Beding. Naturally, the ecophilosophers kept very quiet about this high-level financial agenda behind their journey. Erling, on the other hand, was open about his business with the corrupt Nepalese Royalty, and he amused himself by hiring a helicopter so that he could see with his own eyes what the village of Beding was like, and hand out blankets and clothes to the poor.[73]

The philosophers were not to seek shipping opportunities, but to climb the mountains of an environment in which the people lived in a harmony with nature. It took, in all, twenty-six Sherpa transporters walking for eight days to make this happen, though they tried to keep their climbing equipment to a minimum. When they arrived they were amazed to find people entirely untouched by Western influences. For two months they lived in a true "steady-state community", Kvaløy observed, with "balance and peace between the people and the nature they depended on".[74] To him the lifestyle of Beding was an antidote to the consumer and ecologically destructive societies of the West. The difference between work and leisure, the unfortunate and the élite, and means and ends, were here blurred, as people of Beding strove only for the common good of the village and the environment. It was a "self-supporting society" that "we should envy – especially since we soon will arrive at the bitter end of the eco-crisis", Kvaløy argued.[75] Faarlund was equally convinced: "The 110 inhabitants of Beding knew how we should behave in order to prevent the danger of an ecocatastrophe", he claimed.[76] Similarly, Næss later praised the Sherpa community in his Deep Ecology writings as "an extremely nature-friendly non-violent Buddhist culture in an extremely unwelcoming nature".[77] Indeed, in comparison Næss saw westerners as "worse pests" than leeches attacking his own body.[78] As to their climbing, they decided not to reach for the top of Tseringma out of respect to the locals who thought of it as a holy mountain.[79]

Upon their return to Oslo, they recounted their experiences in three articles for the weekend magazine of the largest newspaper in Norway. For most Norwegians this was their first report about life in Nepal, and the articles mobilized a decade-long longing for Sherpa life, with climbers and tourists using their vacations to follow the footstep of the

gut 2000 Meter Höhe gelegenen Ortschaft Nagarkot aufstiegen, bevor sie in die Heimat zurückkehrten, um die Coworking-Gruppe zum Schutz von Natur und Umwelt sowie die Ökophilosophische Gruppe zu organisieren. Kvaløy reiste im Winter 1969 erneut nach Indien und erklomm auf dem Weg den Damavand im Iran, ihm zur Seite Stein Jarving (geb. 1945), der, von Kvaløys Gedanken begeistert, nach der Rückkehr in die Heimat eine am ökologischen Fließgleichgewicht ausgerichtete landwirtschaftliche Kommune gründete.[70]

Nach zwei Jahren Umweltaktivismus im eigenen Land kehrten Næss und Kvaløy 1971 in den Sommerferien nach Nepal zurück, diesmal mit ihrem Bergsteigergefährten Faarlund. Die Reise sollte eine zweimonatige „Pilgerfahrt" zu dem entlegenen Dorf Beding im nepalesischen Rolwalingtal und ein Urlaub vom „grellen, betäubenden Albtraum" der europäischen „Konsumgesellschaft" sein.[71] Dabei folgten die drei einem weitverbreiteten Trend, nach östlicher Weisheit und alternativen Lebensformen zu suchen. In den frühen 1970er Jahren kamen westliche Hippies zu Tausenden nach Kathmandu, wo sie nahe dem Durbarplatz ihre eigene „Freakstraße" hatten, in der sie unkonventionelle Lebensstile pflegten und auf nepalesische Lebensformen sannen.[72]

Die finanzielle Unterfütterung der Ökophilosophen war weniger exotisch, denn für die Reise zahlte Næss' Halbbruder Erling (1901–93), der mit industriellem Walfang in den 1930er und mit dem Seetransport von Erdöl in den 1960er Jahren ein enormes Vermögen gemacht hatte. Er nahm die Ökophilosophen mit, um Prinz Cayandendra und Maharadscha Mayurbhany, deren persönliche finanzielle Interessen er durch den Aufbau der staatlich subventionierten Royal Nepal Shipping bediente, seiner kulturellen Ehrerbietung gegenüber Nepal zu versichern. Aus Höflichkeit erteilten Prinz und Maharadscha den Ökophilosophen die erforderlichen Reisegenehmigungen, sodass diese das Touristen verschlossene Dorf Beding besuchen konnten. Natürlich schwiegen die Ökophilosophen sich über die ihrer Reise zugrunde liegende hochrangige Finanzagenda aus. Erling dagegen machte keinen Hehl aus seinen Geschäften mit dem korrupten nepalesischen Königshaus und mietete spaßeshalber einen Hubschrauber, um mit eigenen Augen zu sehen, was es mit dem Dorf Beding auf sich hatte, und den Bedürftigen Decken und Kleidung auszuhändigen.[73]

Die Philosophen waren freilich nicht auf Schifffahrtsgeschäfte aus, sondern wollten die Berge in einer Umwelt besteigen, in der die Menschen in Harmonie mit der Natur lebten. Alles in allem brauchten sie dazu 26 Sherpa-Träger und acht Tage, obwohl sie ihre Kletterausrüstung auf das Mindeste zu beschränken versucht hatten. Bei ihrer Ankunft fanden sie zu ihrem Erstaunen von westlichen Einflüssen vollkommen unberührten Menschen vor. Zwei Monate ecophilosophers.[80] Yet the life of the Sherpa did not differ radically from the vanishing class of hardworking fjord and mountain farmers of Norway.[81] What the ecophilosophers' audience saw in their reports from Nepal was thus the superiority of traditional Norwegian mountain and fjord culture which in the 1960s re-emerged in the lifestyle of weekenders' romance with their vacation cottages, many of which were once self-sufficient steady-state farming communities.

Formulating deep ecology

The ecophilosophers returned to Oslo armed with the Oriental wisdom of the Sherpa, along with a new fascination for Buddhism and the Bhagavad-Gita. They received a mixed greeting, as some ecologists found it hard to embrace such religious thinking. Among them were Østbye, Mysterud, and David R. Klein (b. 1923). Klein was an ecologist at the University of Alaska spending his sabbatical year in Oslo from the autumn of 1971 to research reindeer, among other things. Intrigued by the ecophilosophers, he arranged a small seminar with them at Tømte Gård, a botanical Research Station, in February 1972, where he warned against the pitfalls of a new "ecoreligion", as it "will ultimately suffer the same problem of dissolution with the advancement of knowledge as have religions in the past".[82] Instead, he argued, the philosophers should formulate a new eco-ethics or philosophy based on a scientific foundation.

If one is to judge from the subsequent discussions, Klein made an impact. At least, there were no attempts to formulate a new eco-religion based on the ecophilosophers' Oriental experiences, even though Kvaløy personally became a Buddhist. Instead, the Sherpa became a source of inspiration for an alternative ecologically non-anthropocentric rationality.

First out was Faarlund, who concluded that one could not expect to re-educate Western grown-ups in the Oriental wisdom. Instead he put his efforts and hopes in educating the very young in Sherpa lifestyle, as their "eco-life" was "free-air-life" and a viable alternative to the advancing eco-crisis. Only by learning to live inside nature could one build a "bridge from a human-centred (techno-culture) to a humanintegrated way of understanding nature (eco-culture)", he argued.[83]

Kvaløy also saw life in Beding as a viable alternative to the industrial growth society of the Europeans, as he spun into hectic writing in the autumn of 1971. He enlarged and rewrote a previous manuscript about the importance of ecological complexity for social steady-state, in which he argued that harmonious living depended on being within a community with dense biodiversity.[84] This idea evolved into

lang lebten sie in einer echten „Gemeinschaft des Fließgleichgewichts", bemerkte Kvaløy, wo „zwischen den Menschen und der Natur, auf die sie angewiesen waren, Ausgewogenheit und Frieden" herrschte.[74] Für ihn war die Lebensweise von Beding ein Antidot zu den ökologisch destruktiven Konsumgesellschaften des Westens. Die Unterschiede zwischen Arbeit und Freizeit, Benachteiligten und Elite, Mittel und Zweck verschwammen, denn die Menschen in Beding strebten ausschließlich nach dem gemeinsamen Wohl des Dorfes und der Umwelt. Es war eine „selbsttragende Gesellschaft", die „wir beneiden sollten – besonders da wir bald am bitteren Ende der Ökokrise ankommen werden", meinte Kvaløy.[75] Faarlund war gleichermaßen überzeugt: „Die 110 Einwohner von Beding wussten, wie wir uns verhalten sollten, um der Gefahr einer Ökokatastrophe vorzubeugen", behauptete er.[76] Ähnlich lobte Næss in seinen tiefenökologischen Schriften die Sherpa später als „eine äußerst naturfreundliche, gewaltfreie buddhistische Kultur in einer äußerst unwirtlichen Natur".[77] Er erkannte sogar in den Abendländern eine „schlimmere Pest" als in den Blutegeln, die ihm zu Leibe rückten.[78] Was das Klettern anging, sah die Gruppe aus Respekt vor den Einheimischen davon ab, den Gipfel des Tseringma zu erklimmen, weil diese ihn als heiligen Berg verehrten.[79]

Bei ihrer Rückkehr nach Oslo schilderten sie ihre Erlebnisse in drei Artikeln im Wochenendmagazin der größten Zeitung Norwegens. Für die meisten Norweger war dies der erste Bericht über das Leben in Nepal, und die Artikel lösten eine Jahrzehnte währende Sehnsucht nach dem Leben der Sherpa aus, sodass Bergsteiger und Touristen ihre Urlaube nutzten, um in die Fußstapfen der Ökophilosophen zu treten.[80] Doch das Leben der Sherpa unterschied sich gar nicht grundlegend von dem der schwindenden Klasse hart arbeitender Fjord- und Bergbauern in Norwegen.[81] Was die Leserschaft der Ökophilosophen in den Berichten aus Nepal sah, war demnach die Überlegenheit traditioneller norwegischer Berg- und Fjordkultur, die in den 1960er Jahren im liebevollen Verhältnis der Wochenendausflügler zu ihren Ferienhäuschen wieder auftauchte, deren viele einst zu selbstversorgenden, im Fließgleichgewicht arbeitenden landwirtschaftlichen Gemeinschaften gehört hatten.

Die Formulierung der Tiefenökologie

Gerüstet mit der fernöstlichen Weisheit der Sherpa und mit einer neuen Faszination für den Buddhismus und die Bhagavad Gita kehrten die Ökophilosophen nach Oslo zurück. Sie stießen auf ein geteiltes Echo, da es manchen Ökologen schwer vorstellbar schien, sich derlei religiösem Gedankengut anzuschließen, unter ihnen auch Østbye, Mysterud und David R. Klein (geb. 1923). Klein war Ökologe an der Universität Alaska und verbrachte seit Herbst 1971 sein Sabbatjahr in Oslo, unter anderem, um

a larger manuscript in which he argued that such living entailed making an end to industrial society and turning to agrarian living. His model was the Sherpa, whose "settlement in rhythm with the landscape" conveyed "a lifestyle providing lasting security" for their community through "interaction with nature".[85] Such a "life necessities society" was, in comparison with the standardized "industrial growth society", rich in cultural and ecological complexity and should thus be a model for Norwegian interaction with their environment.[86] The breakdown of ecological complexity caused by the Western industrial world would inevitably lead to an eco-catastrophe, he argued, and it was thus urgent to learn from the good people of Beding: "Sherpa and similar societies should be regarded as a vital source of knowledge to us today."[87]

Næss was equally convinced about the virtue of the Sherpa living. His subsequent lectures about ecology and philosophy, held in the autumn of 1971 and spring of 1972, served as evidence of ecological balance's not being "an invention of theoreticians, since it has been and to a certain extent still is praxis today in certain societies, as in the Sherpa communities in Nepal".[88] His earlier endorsement of Maoism was now toned down, by adding that "Mao has *perhaps* kept a part of the classical Chinese outlook" with respect to humans' being fragments in nature.[89] Instead Næss brought Gandhi's principles of non-violence and his own reading of the BhagavadGita to the core of his ecosophy, arguing the individual self was a fragment within the large Self (with a capital S) for the world as a whole. This sense of being a fragment reflected Næss's personal experiences of minuteness when climbing mountains like Tirich Mir, and his meeting with Sherpa lifestyle, as well as the ecologists' research into energy circulation in the Finse region. His ecosophy was, in effect, a philosophy of the Alpine Club by Oriental means.

Internationally, Næss introduced his deep ecology in a paper at the World Future Research Conference in Bucharest in early September 1972. The conference was organized by the World Futures Studies Federation initiated by Galtung and his Peace Research Institute in Oslo, which hosted its inaugural conference in 1967. What dominated Future Studies in 1972 was *The Limits to Growth* report for the Club of Rome written, among others, by the twenty-seven-year-old Norwegian solid-state physicist Jørgen Randers (b. 1945). Randers was at the time entirely unknown: his sole publication was his M.A. thesis of 1969 about the spread of inelastic neutrons.[90] It was therefore a shock to the Norwegian environmentalists to see this nobody rise to world fame, thanks to a public relation firm, Calvin Kyle Associates, which through clever marketing pushed the sale of the report to a total of nine million copies. The public rela-

Rentiere zu erforschen. Auf die Ökophilosophen aufmerksam geworden, arrangierte er im Februar 1972 ein kleines Seminar mit ihnen in der botanischen Forschungsstation Tømte Gård, wo er vor den Fallstricken einer neuen „Ökoreligion" warnte, „weil diese mit fortschreitendem Wissen letztlich ähnliche Verfallsprobleme bekommen wird wie Religionen in der Vergangenheit".[82] Wie er meinte, sollten die Philosophen vielmehr eine neue Öko-Ethik oder Philosophie ausarbeiten, die auf einem wissenschaftlichen Fundament ruhe.

Nach den anschließenden Diskussionen zu gehen, hatte Klein eine gewisse Wirkung erzielt. Zumindest gab es keine Versuche, eine neue Öko-Religion auf Grundlage der Fernost-Erfahrungen der Ökophilosophen zu formulieren, auch wenn Kvaløy persönlich Buddhist geworden war. Stattdessen wurde die Sherpa zu einer Inspirationsquelle für eine alternative, ökologisch nicht-anthropozentrische Rationalität.

Als erster meldete sich Faarlund mit der Einlassung, man könne nicht erwarten, westliche Erwachsene auf östliche Weisheit umzuschulen. Vielmehr setze er seine Bemühungen und Hoffnungen darauf, die ganz Jungen in der Lebensweise der Sherpa zu unterrichten, da deren „Öko-Leben" ein „Freiluftleben" und eine gangbare Alternative zur voranschreitenden Ökokrise sei. Nur wenn man lerne, in der Natur zu leben, könnte man eine „Brücke von einem humanzentrierten (Technokultur) zu einem human-integrierten (Ökokultur) Naturverständnis" schlagen, argumentierte er.[83]

Auch Kvaløy begriff das Leben in Beding als tragfähige Alternative zur industriellen Wachstumsgesellschaft, als er sich im Herbst 1971 in hektische Schreibtätigkeit stürzte. Er erweiterte und überarbeitete ein früheres Manuskript über die Bedeutung ökologischer Komplexität für das soziale Fließgleichgewicht, worin er argumentierte, ein harmonisches Leben sei nur innerhalb einer Gemeinschaft mit hoher Biodiversität möglich.[84] Diesen Gedanken entwickelte er in einem längeren Text weiter, in dem er ausführte, ein solches Leben bedinge, mit der Industriegesellschaft Schluss zu machen und sich einer agrarischen Existenz zuzuwenden. Sein Vorbild waren die Sherpa, deren „auf die Landschaft abgestimmte Siedlungsweise" ihrer Gemeinschaft durch das „Zusammenspiel mit der Natur" ein „Leben in dauerhafter Sicherheit" gewährleiste.[85] Eine solche „Gesellschaft der Lebensnotwendigkeiten" sei im Vergleich zur standardisierten „industriellen Wachstumsgesellschaft" reich an kultureller und ökologischer Komplexität und daher für die Norweger ein Vorbild des Zusammenspiels mit der landeseigenen Umwelt.[86] Der von der westlichen Industriewelt bewirkte Zerfall der ökologischen Komplexität werde unweigerlich zu einer Ökokatastrophe führen, weshalb dringend von den guten Menschen in Beding

tions stunt was financed by the industrialist Aurelio Pecci and the Volkswagen-Foundation, funds which made sure the report dominated environmental debate after its release in March throughout the United Nation's Conference on the Human Environment in Stockholm in June.[91] Though *The Limits to Growth* predicted limits to natural resources, it did not predict limits to existing political systems. The MIT group behind the report was, in this respect, part of a larger trend of environmentalists looking for solutions to ecological problems within established social structures. Most prominent among them was the architect Richard Buckminster Fuller, whose widely read *Operating Manual for Spaceship Earth* (1969) did more than merely hint at an engineering and managerial answer to the ecological crisis. His assistant, John McHale, was a dominating figure in Future Studies circles, arguing that the world did not need a social, spiritual or lifestyle revolution, but instead a technologically-driven design revolution.[92] Rumanian scholars were in majority both as presenters and in the audience, and they were vocal supporters of technocratic solutions to social and environmental ills. Licinius Ciplea, for example, gave a paper entitled "The technological parameters of long range ecological politics", in which he argued that better technologies and social management could mobilize enough natural resources for the whole world.[93] At the opening of the Bucharest conference, the technocrats thus had a leading role in setting up questions and formulating answers to the ecological crisis.

For Galtung and Næss, the time was ripe in Bucharest to hit back at what they saw as a "shallow" technocratic analysis of the environmental situation. Galtung spoke first with his paper *The Limits to Growth and class politics*, a head-on attack on the lack of social analysis in the report. It represented an "ideology of the middle class", he argued, that was "politically blind" to the interest of the poor. Indeed, the Club of Rome-informed recommendations by the Stockholm "conference was staged by 'The International Union of the World's Middle Class'", and one should therefore "fight these cheap and dangerous solutions" in interest of the workers of the world.[94] Galtung had Marxist sympathies. On the wall at the back of the stage on which he was speaking was a mural "to the glory of socialist labour", and the lecture was simultaneously translated into key East Block languages.[95] His class perspective must thus have been welcome to the chief patron of the Bucharest conference, the Romanian President Nicolae Ceaușescu, who saw class-based Future Studies as an integral part of the "Science of Social Management" on which he based his Marxist regime.[96]

When it was Næss's turn to mount the rostrum in Bucharest, he too took an "anticlass posture", but

gelernt werden müsse: „Sherpa und ähnliche Gesellschaften sollten heute als für uns lebenswichtige Wissensquelle betrachtet werden."⁸⁷

Næss war vom Wert der Sherpa-Lebensweise ebenso überzeugt. Seine im Herbst 1971 und Frühjahr 1972 gehaltenen Vorlesungen zur Ökologie und Philosophie dienten zum Beweis, dass ökologische Ausgewogenheit nicht „eine Erfindung von Theoretikern" ist, „da sie gelebte Praxis war und es in gewissem Grade in manchen Gesellschaften bis heute ist, so etwa bei den Sherpa-Gemeinschaften in Nepal".⁸⁸ Seine frühere Befürwortung des Maoismus milderte er nun ab, indem er hervorhob: „Mao hat möglicherweise einen Teil der klassischen chinesischen Sichtweise beibehalten", was das Bild von den Menschen als Fragmenten in der Natur betreffe.⁸⁹ Stattdessen stellte er Gandhis Prinzipien der Gewaltlosigkeit und seine eigene Lesart der Bhagavad Gita ins Zentrum seiner Ökosophie und legte dar, das Individuelle selbst sei ein Fragment innerhalb des großen Selbst (mit groß geschriebenem S), das für die Welt als Ganzes stehe. Ein Fragment zu sein, diese Wahrnehmung widerspiegelte Næss' persönliche Erfahrungen mit der eigenen Winzigkeit, wenn er Berge wie den Tirich Mir bestieg, aber auch seine Begegnung mit der Lebensweise der Sherpa sowie die Forschungen der Ökologen zum Energiekreislauf in der Umgebung von Finse. Seine Ökosophie war im Endeffekt eine Philosophie des Alpenvereins auf fernöstlichem Wege.

Auf internationalem Parkett stellte Næss seine Tiefenökologie Anfang September 1972 in einem Vortrag auf der World Future Research Conference in Bukarest vor. Die Konferenz organisierten der von Galtung initiierte Weltverband für Zukunftsforschung und das ebenfalls von Galtung gegründete Osloer Friedensforschungsinstitut, das die Eröffnungskonferenz im Jahr 1967 beherbergt hatte. 1972 wurde die Zukunftsforschung beherrscht vom Bericht des Club of Rome über *Die Grenzen des Wachstums*, den neben anderen der 27 Jahre alte norwegische Fließgleichgewichts-Physiker Jørgen Randers (geb. 1945) verfasst hatte. Randers war zu diesem Zeitpunkt völlig unbekannt: Seine einzige Publikation war eine Magisterarbeit über inelastische Neutronenstreuung aus dem Jahr 1969.⁹⁰ Deshalb war es ein Schock für die norwegischen Umweltforscher, dass dieser Niemand zu Weltruhm aufstieg – dank einer Public-Relations-Firma, Calvin Kyle Associates, die den Verkauf des Berichts durch cleveres Marketing auf insgesamt neun Millionen Exemplare hochtrieb. Finanziert wurde der Werbecoup von dem Industriellen Aurelio Pecci und der VolkswagenStiftung – Investitionen, die sicherstellten, dass der Bericht nach seiner Veröffentlichung im März die Umweltdiskussionen auf der Stockholmer Konferenz der Vereinten Nationen über die Umwelt des Menschen im Juni vollständig beherrschte.⁹¹ Nun prognostizierte *Die Grenzen des Wachstums* zwar die Begrenztheit

would otherwise stay away from socialist lingo in presenting "The Shallow and the Deep Ecology Movement" in Norway. It was immediately understood as an onslaught on the "shallow" technocratic perspective of Randers and the Club of Rome. This "restricted movement which has many friends among the power élite", Næss argued, was in danger of consolidating the debate at the expense of "the deeper movement [which] finds itself in danger of being deceived through smart manoeuvres".⁹⁷ That there thus were two ecological movements was controversial to Ceaușescu's followers, who could see only one movement towards one future. Much of the debate at the conference would centre on this point. Næss would, as a consequence, change the title of his paper from "movement" to "movements" to emphasize pluralism of possible ecological perspectives, and he borrowed the words "Long Range" from Ciplea to indicate that the future could entail answers to ecological problems other than Ceaușescu's socialist technocracy. Strangely, no evidence suggests that the most original aspect of the paper, the eco-centrism, raised any interest. As argued above, this perspective emerged from a culture of outdoor lifestyle among Norwegian ecologists, or as Næss put it: "Ecological insight and the lifestyle of the ecological field-worker have *suggested, inspired, and fortified* the perspectives of the deep ecology movement."⁹⁸

Ironically, the long-range ecology movement Næss spoke of would fade upon his return to Oslo, as the Co-working Group for the Protection of Nature and the Environment was infiltrated and taken over by Marxist Leninists. It died away in 1973 after a period of internal cleansings and futile debates about the value of democracy.⁹⁹ Its last unified stand came with the national referendum on membership in the European Community at the end of September 1972. They were decisively against, arguing that "this industrial-serving mega-society seeks to break apart the established *diversity* of sturdy self-governed and heterogeneously, traditional-coloured local communities, – and replace them with a uniform system of government that presupposes uniform social units and a uniform culture: a simplification that increases vulnerability, according to the science of ecology".¹⁰⁰ They won their case, as Norway voted against membership, but could not decide on what to do next. As a result, the Ecophilosophy Group became divided into a socialist and an ecological wing. Mysterud was the first to notice this leftward turn in the politics of ecology, something he regretted as it undermined the broad science-based environmentalism he sought to mobilize.¹⁰¹ Faarlund, Kvaløy and Næss agreed. They continued with their activities, together with former activists, in various environmental organizations and groupings outside the University of

natürlicher Ressourcen, nicht aber die Begrenztheit bestehender politischer Systeme. Die hinter dem Bericht stehende MIT-Gruppe folgte in dieser Hinsicht einem allgemeineren Trend vieler Ökologen, die Lösung ökologischer Probleme innerhalb etablierter gesellschaftlicher Strukturen zu suchen. Ein äußerst prominenter Vertreter dieser Richtung war der Architekt Richard Buckminster Fuller, dessen viel gelesene *Bedienungsanleitung für das Raumschiff Erde* (1969) mehr tat, als nur eine ingenieursmäßige und verfahrenstechnische Antwort auf die ökologische Krise zu umreißen. Sein Assistent John McHale, eine tonangebende Figur in Zukunftsforscherkreisen, argumentierte, die Welt brauche keine gesellschaftliche, geistige oder lebensartliche Revolution, sondern vielmehr eine technologisch gesteuerte Gestaltungsrevolution.[92] Rumänische Wissenschaftler waren als Vortragende wie im Publikum in der Mehrheit, und sie unterstützten lautstark technologische Lösungen für Missstände in Gesellschaft und Umwelt. Licinius Ciplea zum Beispiel hielt ein Referat über „Technologische Parameter langfristiger ökologischer Politik", in dem er die Ansicht vertrat, bessere Technologien und besseres Sozialmanagement könnten genügend natürliche Ressourcen für die ganze Welt bereitstellen.[93] Bei der Eröffnung der Bukarester Konferenz hatten die Technokraten demnach eine führende Rolle bezüglich der Fragestellungen und der Formulierung von Antworten auf die ökologische Krise.

Für Galtung und Næss war in Bukarest die Zeit gekommen, auf die nach ihrer Auffassung „seichte" Analyse der Umweltsituation zu kontern. Als erster ergriff Galtung in seinem Referat *Die Grenzen des Wachstums und Klassenpolitik* das Wort, worin er einen Frontalangriff auf die fehlende Gesellschaftsanalyse im Bericht des Club of Rome führte. Dieser repräsentiere eine „Ideologie der Mittelschicht", die für die Interessen der Armen „politisch blind" sei. Tatsächlich wurden die Club-of-Rome-geprägten Empfehlungen der Stockholmer Konferenz „durch die ‚International Union of the World's Middle Class' vorgetragen", weshalb man im Interesse der Arbeiter in aller Welt „solche billigen und gefährlichen Lösungen" bekämpfen müsse.[94] Galtung sympathisierte mit dem Marxismus. Auf der Rückwand der Bühne, auf der er sprach, befand sich ein Bild „zum Lob der sozialistischen Arbeit", und der Vortrag wurde simultan in wichtige Ostblocksprachen gedolmetscht.[95] Seine Klassenperspektive muss dem Hauptschirmherrn der Bukarester Konferenz, dem rumänischen Präsidenten Nicolae Ceauşescu, willkommen gewesen sein, der klassenorientierte Zukunftsforschung als integralen Bestandtteil seiner „Wissenschaft vom Sozialmanagement" betrachtete, auf die er sein marxistisches Regime stützte.[96]

Als Næss das Bukarester Podium betrat, sah auch er eine „Klassenfeindschaft" für gegeben an, hielt sich aber ansonsten vom sozialistischen Jargon

Oslo, where they, among other things, published key anthologies and the first Norwegian environmental encyclopaedia.[102] Others chose to "drop out" completely by living according to the teaching in Sherpa-style steady-state agricultural communities in old mountain or fjord-farms.[103]

A romance with the cottage gone native

When the young and politically inexperienced feminist Gro Harlem Brundtland (b. 1939) became Minister of the Environment in 1974, she would face environmental activists and philosophers mentioned in this article in various heated debates and rough conflicts. They used every opportunity to show that the ecological steadystate society was "not an herbal-tea party", but a revolutionary break with industrial growth.[104] As a medical doctor she would take a strictly anthropocentric stand against them as well as against ecologists claiming to speak on behalf of nature, arguing that only human bureaucratic rules and democratic procedures should be hailed.[105] Yet in offering resistance to her views, both the ecophilosophers and the ecologists forced Brundtland to reflect more deeply on social aspects of environmental affairs, as she later did in *Our Common Future* (1987).

In the meantime the ecophilosophers hardened their thinking, and the group became increasingly fundamentalist. As Næss later admitted, deep ecology became, in its radicalism, "too narrow – a kind of sect".[106] The ecologists too became increasingly gloomy about how humans should work with nature, as their scientific advice on what to do and how to live in ecological harmony evolved from a culture of vacation which saw the land as a place of leisure. When the Norwegian contribution to the International Biological Programme faded out in 1974, it also marked an end to steady-state ecological research inspired by the Odum brothers. Some ecologists left the field and became teachers or environmental bureaucrats, while those who remained on campus would turn their focus towards evolutionary ecology and sociobiology. Yet ideas about ecological steady-state would develop among the ecophilosophers, whose notions about working with (and not against) nature were modelled on the traditional mountain and fjord-farms taken over by the cottager on vacation. Emerging from this context, deep ecology was a romance with the cottage gone native.

Acknowledgments

I would like to thank John Peter Collett, Robert Marc Friedman, and two anonymous reviewers for thoughtful comments. I have also benefited from talking to Nils Faarlund, Ivar Mysterud, Arne Næss, Jørgen Randers, Sigmund Kvaløy Setereng, and Nils

fern, als er sein Referat „Die Seichtigkeit und die tiefenökologische Bewegung" in Norwegen vortrug. Es wurde sofort als Attacke auf die „seichte" technokratische Perspektive Randers' und des Club of Rome verstanden. Diese „beschränkte Bewegung, die viele Freunde in der Machtelite hat", so Næss, laufe Gefahr, die Debatte festzuklopfen zu Lasten „der tiefer greifenden Bewegung, [die] ihrerseits in Gefahr steht, durch schlaue Manöver hintergangen zu werden".[97] Dass es mithin zwei ökologische Bewegungen gab, war nicht im Sinne der Ceauşescu-Anhänger, die nur eine Bewegung in die Zukunft erkennen konnten. Große Teile der Debatte auf der Konferenz drehten sich um diesen Punkt. Deshalb veränderte Næss den Titel seines Referats von „Bewegung" zu „Bewegungen", um den Pluralismus möglicher ökologischer Perspektiven hervorzuheben, und entlehnte von Ciplea den Begriff „langfristig", um darauf aufmerksam zu machen, dass die Zukunft andere Antworten auf ökologische Probleme erbringen könne als die sozialistische Technokratie Ceausescus. Merkwürdigerweise deutet nichts darauf hin, dass der originellste Aspekt seines Referats, der Ökozentrismus nämlich, irgendein Interesse erweckt hätte. Wie weiter oben dargelegt, erwuchs diese Perspektive eben aus einer Kultur des Freilandlebens unter den norwegischen Ökologen, oder, wie Næss formulierte: „Ökologische Einsicht und die Lebensweise des ökologischen Feldforschers haben die Perspekiven der tiefenökologischen Bewegung angeregt, beflügelt und bestärkt."[98]

Ironischerweise sollte die Bewegung zu einer langfristigen Ökologie, von der Næss sprach, nach seiner Rückkehr nach Oslo einschlafen, weil die Coworking-Gruppe zum Schutz von Natur und Umwelt von Marxisten-Leninisten infiltriert und übernommen wurde. Nach einer Periode interner Säuberungen und müßiger Debatten über den Wert der Demokratie schied sie 1973 dahin.[99] Ihre letzte einmütige Stellungnahme gab sie Ende September 1972 beim nationalen Referendum zur Mitgliedschaft in der Europäischen Gemeinschaft ab. Sie war eindeutig dagegen, da diese „der Industrie dienende Mega-Gesellschaft versucht, die bewährte Diversität stabiler selbstverwalteter und in unterschiedlicher Weise traditionell gefärbter örtlicher Gemeinschaften zu zerbrechen und sie zu ersetzen durch ein einheitliches Regierungssystem, das einheitliche soziale Körperschaften und eine einheitliche Kultur voraussetzt: eine Vereinfachung, die gemäß der Wissenschaft der Ökologie die Anfälligkeit erhöht".[100] Sie gewann den Streit – Norwegen stimmte gegen die Mitgliedschaft –, wusste aber nicht, wie es weitergehen sollte. Infolgedessen spaltete die Ökophilosophische Gruppe sich in einen sozialistischen und einen ökologischen Flügel. Mysterud bemerkte als erster den Linksrutsch in der Ökologiepolitik, den er bedauerte, da dieser den breit angelegten wis-

---

Christian Stenseth, who do not necessarily agree with my reading of all the events.

All translations, unless otherwise noted, are mine.
Anker, Peder
Science As a Vacation: A History of Ecology in Norway
History of Science, volume 45, number 4, december 2007
Science History Publications Ltd.

[1] Max Weber, *Science As a Vocation*, in Peter Lassman, Irving Velody and Herminio Martins (eds), *Max Weber's Science As a Vocation* (London, 1989), 3–31, pp. 18, 27. Originally published as *Wissenschaft als Beruf*, in 1919. Cf. Steven Shapin, Science As a Vocation: *Technical knowledge and personal virtue in late modernity* (forthcoming).

[2] Richard White, "'Are You an Environmentalist or Do You Work for Living?': Work and Nature", in William Cronon (ed.), *Uncommon Ground* (New York, 1995), pp. 171–85.

[3] Weber, "Science As a Vocation" (ref. 1), 30; idem, *The Protestant Ethic and the Spirit of Capitalism* (New York, 1930).

[4] Charles P. Snow, *The Two Cultures and the Scientific Revolution* (Cambridge, 1959). On the history of the University of Oslo see John Peter Collett, *Historien om Universitetet i Oslo* (Oslo, 1999).

[5] The most comprehensive anthology of articles from this period is the excellent collection of Peter Reed and David Rothenberg (eds), *Wisdom in the open air: The Norwegian roots of deep ecology*, Minneapolis, 1993. See also David Rothenberg, *Is it painful to think? Conversations with Arne Næss*, Minneapolis, 1993; and Ron Eyerman, "Intellectuals and popular movements: The Alta confrontation in Norway", in *Praxis international*, iii (1983), pp. 185–98. For a parallel history in Sweden see Klas Sandell and Sverker Sörlin (eds), *Frliluftshistoria: Från 'härdande friluftslif' till ekoturism och miljöpedagogik* (Stocholm, 2000); and Thomas Söderqvist, *The ecologists: From merry naturalists to saviours of the nation, a sociologically informed narrative survey of the ecologization of Sweden* (Stockholm, 1986). See also Pascal Acot, *Histoire de l'écologie* (Paris, 1988); Fredrick Buell, *From apocalypse to way of life* (New York, 2003); Stephen Bocking, *Ecologists and environmental politics* (New Haven, 1997); Frank Benjamin Golley, *A history of the ecosystem concept in ecology* (New Haven, 1993); Joel B. Hagen, *An entangled bank* (New Brunswick, 1992); Sharon E. Kingsland, *The evolution of American ecology 1890–2000* (Baltimore, 2005); Robert E. Kohler, *Landscapes and labscapes* (Chicago, 2002); Gregg Mitman, *Reel nature* (Cambridge, MA, 1999); Douglas Weiner, *A little corner of freedom* (Berkeley, 1999); and Donald Worster, *Nature's economy*, 2nd edn (Cambridge, 1994).

senschaftlich fundierten Umweltgedanken, den er befördern wollte, untergrub.[101] Faarlund, Kvaløy und Næss stimmten ihm zu. Gemeinsam mit früheren Aktivisten setzten sie ihre Tätigkeiten in verschiedenen Umweltorganisationen und Gruppen außerhalb der Universität Oslo fort und publizierten unter anderem entscheidende Anthologien sowie die erste norwegische Umwelt-Enzyklopädie.[102] Andere „stiegen komplett aus" und lebten gemäß der Lehre von agrarischen Gemeinschaften nach dem Vorbild der auf das Fließgleichgewicht ausgerichteten Sherpa in alten Berg- oder Fjordbauernhöfen.[103]

Eine Romanze mit dem Ferienhaus der rückbesinnlichen Art

Als die junge und politisch unerfahrene Feministin Gro Harlem Brundtland (geb. 1939) 1974 norwegische Umweltministerin wurde, hatte sie so manche hitzige Debatten und scharfe Konflikte mit den erwähnten Aktivisten und Philosophen auszufechten. Diese nutzten jede Gelegenheit, um zu beweisen, dass die ökologische Gesellschaft des Fließgleichgewichts „kein Kräutertee-Kränzchen" war, sondern eine revolutionäre Abkehr vom industriellen Wachstum bedeutete.[104] Als Ärztin bezog Brundtland ihnen gegenüber wie auch gegenüber Ökologen, die im Namen der Natur zu sprechen beanspruchten, einen strikt anthropozentrischen Standpunkt und ließ nur menschliche Verfahrensregeln und demokratische Beschlussweisen als lobenswert gelten.[105] Indem die Ökophilosophen und Ökologen Brundtlands Ansichten Widerstand entgegensetzten, zwangen sie die Politikerin jedoch zu einer eingehenderen Beschäftigung mit den sozialen Aspekten von Umweltfragen, wie sie sie später in *Unsere gemeinsame Zukunft* (1987) geleistet hat.

In der Zwischenzeit härteten die Ökophilosophen ihr Denken, und die Gruppe wurde zunehmend fundamentalistischer. Wie Næss später einräumte, wurde die Tiefenökologie in ihrem Radikalismus „allzu engstirnig – eine Art Sekte".[106] Auch die Ökologen sahen immer schwärzer in der Frage, wie die Menschen mit der Natur arbeiten sollten, da ihr wissenschaftlicher Rat, was zu tun und wie in ökologischer Harmonie zu leben sei, aus einer Urlaubskultur erwuchs, der das Land als Freizeitgelände galt. Als die norwegische Beteiligung am Internationalen Biologischen Programm 1974 auslief, bedeutete dies auch das Ende der durch die Odum-Brüder angeregten ökologischen Erforschung des Fließgleichgewichts. Einige Ökologen wanderten in andere Berufsfelder ab und wurden Lehrer oder Umweltbürokraten, während diejenigen, die auf dem Campus verblieben, sich schwerpunktmäßig der Evolutionsökologie und der Soziobiologie zuwandten. Weiterentwickelt wurden die Ideen zum ökologischen Fließgleichgewicht jedoch unter den Ökophilosophen, deren Vorstellungen, mit der (und nicht gegen die) Natur zu arbeiten, den traditionel-

---

[6] Central Bureau of Statistics, *Holiday house survey* (Oslo, 1967/1968, 1970); *Outdoor life* (Oslo, 1970, 1974); and *Holiday survey* (Oslo, 1968).

[7] Bredo Berntsen, "Nasjonalparker", in *Naturen*, xcvi (1972), pp. 195–204; idem, *Naturvernets historie i Norge: Fra klassisk naturvern til økopolitikk* (Oslo, 1977); idem, *Grønne linjer: Natur og miljøvernets historie i Norge* (Oslo, 1994), pp. 114–76; idem, *Norsk natur og miljøvernlitteratur 1908–1980 : En annotert bibliografi* (Oslo, 1982); anonymous (ed.), *Miljøvern og kraftutbygging* (Oslo, 1970); Olav G. Henriksen (ed.), *Kvinner i fjellet* (Lom, 2002); Gunnar Repp, "Norwegian relationships to nature through outdoor life", in Jan Neuman, Ivar Mytting and Jiri Brtnik (eds), *Outdoor activities* (Lüneburg, 1996), pp. 32–42; Alf-Inge Jansen, *Makt og miljø: En studie av utformingen av den statlige natur og miljøvernpolitikken* (Oslo, 1989), pp. 51–101; Eivind Dale, Hilde Jervan, Atle Midttun, Jan Eivind Myhre and Dag Namtvedt, *Ressursforvaltningens historie* (Oslo, 1984), pp. 35–84; and Ulf Hafsten, in *Naturvernets århundre* (Oslo, 1977).

[8] Eilif Dahl, *Økopolitikk og økologi* (Oslo, 1971), p. 9; idem, "Miljøforskning, produktforskning og prioriteringen av oppgavene", in *Forskningsnytt*, iv (1968), pp. 65–67; Sigmund Huse, "Naturvern på økologisk grunnlag", in *Norsk natur*, i (1965), pp. 4–7; and Gunnar Lid, "Om dyrelivet i den foreslåtte nasjonalparken på Hardangervidda", in *Norsk natur*, ii (1966), pp. 66–71.

[9] Thor Larsen, "Økologi og sunn fornuft", *Norsk natur*, vii (1971), pp. 40–41. Larsen was a marine biologist at the University of Oslo.

[10] Eivind Østbye, "Høyfjellsøkologisk forskningsstasjons historie", in *Finse: Et senter for høyfjellsforskning* (Finse, 1997), pp. 3–9; idem, *Bibliography of the Finse area 1781–1996* (Finse, 1997); and Finn R. Jørstad, *Historien om Finse* (Bergen, 1998).

[11] 'Ecology' as a term had only been in intramural use among social anthropologists, most notably Fredrik Barth who introduced human ecological perspectives in Norway. Helge Kleivan, "Økologisk endring i Labrador", in *Naturen*, lxxxvi (1962), pp. 200–13, note 1.

[12] Eilif Dahl, *Forelesninger i økologi* (Ås, 1966); Eugene P. Odum, *Fundamentals of ecology*, 2nd edn (Philadelphia, 1959); and H. M. Thamdrup, *Naturens husholdning* (Oslo, 1966).

[13] Eivind Østbye, "Aktuell forskning i enkle økosystemer, med særlig henblikk på høyfjellsforskning I Norge", in *Forskningsnytt*, iv (1967), pp. 70–73.

[14] Robert E. Kohler, *All creatures: Naturalists, collectors and biodiversity, 1850–1950* (Princeton, 2006), p. 92.

[15] Nils Borchgrevink, "Naturfølelse og naturvern", in *Samtiden*, lxxvii (1968), pp. 360–6, see pp. 360, 361; Arne B. Johansen, "Hardangervidda skal utforskes: Et prosjekt for tverrvitenskaplig

len, unterdessen von urlaubenden Ferienhäuslern übernommenen Berg- und Fjordbauernhöfen nachempfunden waren. Aus diesem Zusammenhang erwachsen, war die Tiefenökologie eine Romanze mit dem Ferienhaus der rückbesinnlichen Art.

Danksagungen
Peter Collett, Robert Marc Friedman und zwei anonym bleibenden Lektoren möchte für ihre aufmerksamen Kommentare danken. Profitiert habe ich außerdem von Gesprächen mit Nils Faarlund, Ivar Mysterud, Arne Næss, Jørgen Randers, Sigmund Kvaløy Setereng und Nils Christian Stenseth, die mit meiner Lesart der Ereignisse nicht unbedingt übereinstimmen.

Anker, Peder
Science As a Vacation: A History of Ecology in Norway
History of Science, Bd. 45, Nr. 4, Dezember 2007
Science History Publications Ltd.

[1] Max Weber, *Wissenschaft als Beruf*, in: Schriften 1894–1922, ausgewählt und herausgegeben von Dirk Kaesler, Stuttgart 2002, S. 495 bzw. 506.

[2] Richard White, „'Are you an environmentalist or do you work for living?': Work and nature", in: William Cronon (Hrsg.), *Uncommon ground* (New York, 1995), S. 171–85.

[3] Max Weber, *Wissenschaft als Beruf*, a.a.O., S. 510.

[4] Charles P. Snow, *The two cultures and the Scientific Revolution* (Cambridge, 1959). Zur Geschichte der Universität Oslo vgl. John Peter Collett, *Historien om Universitetet i Oslo* (Oslo, 1999).

[5] Die umfassendste Anthologie von Artikeln aus diesem Zeitraum bietet die ausgezeichnete Sammlung von Peter Reed und David Rothenberg (Hrsg.), *Wisdom in the open air: The Norwegian roots of deep ecology*, Minneapolis, 1993. Siehe auch David Rothenberg, *Is it painful to think? Conversations with Arne Næss*, (Minneapolis, 1993), und Ron Eyerman, „Intellectuals and popular movements: The Alta confrontation in Norway", in: *Praxis international*, iii (1983), S. 185–98. Zu einer parallelen Geschichte in Schweden siehe Klas Sandell und Sverker Sörlin (Hrsg.), *Frliluftshistoria: Från 'härdande friluftslif' till ekoturism och miljöpedagogik* (Stockholm, 2000); und Thomas Söderqvist, *The ecologists: From merry naturalists to saviours of the nation, a sociologically informed narrative survey of the ecologization of Sweden* (Stockholm, 1986). Siehe auch Pascal Acot, *Histoire de l'écologie* (Paris, 1988); Fredrick Buell, *From apocalypse to way of life* (New York, 2003); Stephen Bocking, *Ecologists and environmental politics* (New Haven, 1997); Frank Benjamin Golley, *A history of the ecosystem concept in ecology* (New Haven, 1993); Joel B. Hagen, *An entangled bank* (New Brunswick, 1992); Sharon E. Kingsland, *The evolution of American ecology 1890–2000* (Baltimore, 2005); Robert E. Kohler, *Landscapes*

kulturforskning i gang fra 1970", in *Forskningsnytt*, xiv (1969), pp. 26–29; and Anders Hagen, "Fra Hardangervidda historie", in *Forskningsnytt*, xv (1970), pp. 31–35.

[16] Arne Næss, "The conquest of mountains: A contradiction?" [1970], in *Trumpeter*, xxi (2005), pp. 55–56; and Peder Anker, "The philosopher's cabin and the house hold of nature", in *Ethics, place and environment*, vi (2003), pp. 131–41.

[17] Peter Wessel Zapffe, *Barske glæder*, ed. by Sigmund Kvaløy (Oslo, 1969); and Sigmund Kvaløy, "Peter Wessel Zapffe og verdien av utemmet natur", in Guttorm Fløistad and Per Fredrik Christiansen (eds), P. W. Zapffe: *Dikt og drama* (Oslo, 1970), pp. 252–65.

[18] Nils Faarlund, *Friluftsliv: Hva – hvorfor – hvordan* (Oslo, 1973), p. 11; and Nils Faarlund, "Hva mener vi med friluftsliv?", *Mestre fjellet*, xv (1973), pp. 4–6.

[19] Arne Næss, "The Norwegian roots of deep ecology", in Børge Dahle (ed.), *Nature: The true home of culture* (Oslo, 1994), pp. 15–19; Nils Faarlund, "Hva mener vi med friluftsliv?", in *Mestre fjellet*, xv (1973), pp. 4–6; idem, "Friluftsliv – A Way Home", in Børge Dahle (ed.), *Nature: The true home of culture* (Oslo, 1994), pp. 21–26; and Sigmund Kvaløy Setereng, "Inside nature", ibid., pp. 29–37, 1973

[20] Sigmund Kvaløy, *Musikk-kritikk og kommunikasjon* (Oslo, 1965); and Nils Faarlund, "Sigmund 70 år!", *Tindeposten*, iv (2004), pp. 16–19.

[21] Weber, *Science As a Vocation* (ref. 1), p 21.

[22] Eivind Østbye et al., "Hardangervidda, Norway", in *Ecological bulletins*, xx (1975), pp. 225–64; and Eilif Dahl, "Globale ressursproblemer", in *Samtiden*, lxxxii (1973), pp. 257–67.

[23] Torstein Engelskjøn, *Biologisk forskning i Norge: En analyse med spesiell vekt på grunnforskningens ressurser, organisasjon og innhold* (Oslo, 1972), pp. 7–8, pp. 39–40.

[24] Ragnhild Sundby, "Globalforgiftning", in *Naturen*, lxxxix (1965), pp. 3–11; Rachel Carson, *Silent Spring* (Greenwich, 1962); and idem, *Den tause våren* (Oslo, 1962).

[25] Rolf Vik, "Hvor står biologene i teknikkens århundre?", in *Naturen*, xci (1967), pp. 259–69, see p. 269; Georg Henrik von Wright, "Essay om naturen, mennesket og den vitenskaplig-tekniske revolusjon", in *Naturen*, xci (1967), pp. 155–80; Jaques Yves Cousteau, "Er klokken blitt tolv?", in *Naturen*, xciv (1970), pp. 411–20; Lynn White, "Den økologiske krises historiske røtter", in *Naturen*, xcv (1971), pp. 77–92; Brunjulf Valum (ed. and transl.), *Øko-katastrofe: Artikler fra det amerikanske tidsskrift Ramparts med to tillegg om Mardøla-saken* (Oslo, 1971); and Bjørn L. Hegseth, *Miljøkunnskap – miljøvern: Forsøk på en oversikt* (Trondheim, 1970).

[26] Chunglin Kwa, "Representations of nature mediating between ecology and science policy:

and labscapes (Chicago, 2002); Gregg Mitman, *Reel nature* (Cambridge, MA, 1999); Douglas Weiner, *A little corner of freedom* (Berkeley, 1999); und Donald Worster, *Nature's economy*, zweite Ausgabe (Cambridge, 1994).

[6] Central Bureau of Statistics, *Holiday house survey* (Oslo, 1967/1968, 1970); *Outdoor life* (Oslo, 1970, 1974); und *Holiday survey* (Oslo, 1968).

[7] Bredo Berntsen, „Nasjonalparker", in: *Naturen*, xcvi (1972), S. 195–204; ders., *Naturvernets historie i Norge: Fra klassisk naturvern til økopolitikk* (Oslo, 1977); ders., *Grønne linjer: Natur og miljøvernets historie i Norge* (Oslo, 1994), S. 114–76; ders., *Norsk natur og miljøvernlitteratur 1908–1980 : En annotert bibliografi* (Oslo, 1982); N.N. (Hrsg.), *Miljøvern og kraftutbygging* (Oslo, 1970); Olav G. Henriksen (Hrsg.), *Kvinner i fjellet* (Lom, 2002); Gunnar Repp, „Norwegian relationships to nature through outdoor life", in: Jan Neuman, Ivar Mytting und Jiri Brtnik (Hrsg.), *Outdoor activities* (Lüneburg, 1996), S. 32–42; Alf-Inge Jansen, *Makt og miljø: En studie av utformingen av den statlige natur og miljøvernpolitikken* (Oslo, 1989), S. 51–101; Eivind Dale, Hilde Jervan, Atle Midttun, Jan Eivind Myhre und Dag Namtvedt, *Ressursforvaltningens historie* (Oslo, 1984), S. 35–84; und Ulf Hafsten, in: *Naturvernets århundre* (Oslo, 1977).

[8] Eilif Dahl, *Økopolitikk og økologi* (Oslo, 1971), S. 9; ders., „Miljøforskning, produktforskning og prioriteringen av oppgavene", in: *Forskningsnytt*, iv (1968), S. 65–67; Sigmund Huse, „Naturvern på økologisk grunnlag", in: *Norsk natur*, i (1965), S. 4–7; und Gunnar Lid, „Om dyrelivet i den foreslåtte nasjonalparken på Hardangervidda", in: *Norsk natur*, ii (1966), S. 66–71.

[9] Thor Larsen, „Økologi og sunn fornuft", *Norsk natur*, vii (1971), S. 40–41. Larsen war Meeresbiologe an der Universität Oslo.

[10] Eivind Østbye, „Høyfjellsøkologisk forskningsstasjons historie", in *Finse: Et senter for høyfjellsforskning* (Finse, 1997), S. 3–9; ders., *Bibliography of the Finse area 1781–1996* (Finse, 1997); und Finn R. Jørstad, *Historien om Finse* (Bergen, 1998).

[11] »Ökologie« war unter Sozialanthropologen nur ein intern gebrauchter Begriff, besonders bei Fredrik Barth, der humanökologische Perspektiven in Norwegen eingeführt hat. Helge Kleivan, „Økologisk endring i Labrador",in: *Naturen*, lxxxvi (1962), S. 200–13, Anm. 1.

[12] Eilif Dahl, *Forelesninger i økologi* (Ås, 1966); Eugene P. Odum, *Fundamentals of ecology*, zweite Auflage (Philadelphia, 1959); und H. M. Thamdrup, *Naturens husholdning* (Oslo, 1966).

[13] Eivind Østbye, „Aktuell forskning i enkle økosystemer, med særlig henblikk på høyfjellsforskning I Norge", in: *Forskningsnytt*, iv (1967), S. 70–73.

[14] Robert E. Kohler, *All creatures: Naturalists, collectors and biodiversity, 1850–1950* (Princeton, 2006), S. 92.

[15] Nils Borchgrevink, „Naturfølelse og naturvern", in:

The case of the International Biological Programme", *Social studies of science*, xvii (1987), pp. 413–42; and Edgar B. Worthington (ed.), *The evolution of IBP* (Cambridge, 1975).

[27] Rolf Vik, *International Biological Programme: Final report Scandinavian countries* (Oslo, 1975), p. 7; International Biological Programme, *IBP i Norge: Årsrapport* (Oslo, 1968–74); and F. E. Wielgolaski, "Fenologi, produksjonsøkologi og andre kjente eller ukjente økologiske begreper", in *Naturen*, xcii (1968), pp. 179–84.

[28] Rolf Vik and F. E. Wielgolaski, "Det Internationale Biologiske Program i 1969", in *Forskingsnytt*, xv (1970), pp. 14–20, see pp. 14, 16.

[29] Knut Fægri, "Den klassiske biologis stilling i moderne naturvitenskap", *Naturen*, xc (1966), pp. 528–46, see pp. 531, 540; and Nils Roll-Hansen, *Det Internasjonale Biologiske Program (IBP) i Norge* (Oslo, 1982).

[30] Rolf Vik, "Naturvern er menneksevern", in *Naturen*, xc (1966), pp. 195–205, see p. 195; and idem, "Hvor står biologien I teknikkens århundre?", in *Forskningsnytt*, xi (1966), pp. 16–19.

[31] Eilif Dahl quoted in anonymous (ed.), *Working meeting on analysis of ecosystems: Tundra zone* (Ustaoset, 1968), p. 7. Similarly in Arne Semb-Johansson, "Samspillet i naturen", in Ragnar Frislid and Aren Semb-Johansson (eds), *Norges dyr* (Oslo, 1971), v, pp. 44–58.

[32] Anonymous (ed.), *Working meeting* (ref. 31), 32.

[33] Olav Gjærevoll, "Forord", in Nalle Valtiala, *Mennesket – et skadedyr?* (Oslo, 1970), pp. 7–8.

[34] Anonymous, "'Aksjon Hardangervidda' i gang", in *Norsk natur*, vi (1970), pp. 122–4; and Jan Økland, "Naturviten og naturbruk: Om dyreliv og miljøforhold I norske vassdrag", in *Naturen*, xci (1967), pp. 387–97.

[35] Olav R. Skage, *Hardangervidda: Naturvern – kraftutbygging* (Oslo, 1971), 9. Skage summarized unpublished reports by Arne Semb-Johnsson, A. Løvlie, K. Elgmor, Ivar Mysterud, and Eivind Østbye. Ivar Mysterud and Eivind Østbye, "Vitenskaplige interesser og vassdragsreguleringer på Hardangervidda", in *Forsknignsnytt*, i (1972), pp. 35–45; and idem, "The future of Hardangervidda", in *Research in Norway*, i (1973), pp. 57–68.

[36] Rolf Vik, "Forord", in *Vassdrag og samfunn*, ed. by Rolf Vik (Oslo, 1971), 11; and idem, "Vårt miljø og biologenes ansvar", *Samtiden*, lxxviii (1969), 67–69.

[37] Hans Skjervheim, "Naturvern og politikk", Øyvind Østerud, "Naturverdier og samfunn – en ideologisk skisse", and Gunnar Skirbekk, "Distrikshøgskolar, mot-ekspertise og populisme", in *Vassdrag og samfunn*, ed. by Rolf Vik (Oslo, 1971), pp. 180–8, pp. 189–210, pp. 213–34, see p. 181; and Per S. Enger, "Hva nå med norsk biologi?", in Nils Roll-Hansen and Hans Skoie (eds), *Forskningspolitiske spørsmål i norsk biologi* (Oslo, 1974), pp. 86–96.

Samtiden, lxxvii (1968), S. 360–6, hier S. 360, 361; Arne B. Johansen, „Hardangervidda skal utforskes: Et prosjekt for tverrvitenskaplig kulturforskning i gang fra 1970", in: *Forskningsnytt*, xiv (1969), S. 26–29; und Anders Hagen, „Fra Hardangervidda historie", in: *Forskningsnytt*, xv (1970), S. 31–35.

[16] Arne Næss, „The conquest of mountains: A contradiction?" [1970], in: *Trumpeter*, xxi (2005), S. 55–56; und Peder Anker, „The philosopher's cabin and the house hold of nature", in: *Ethics, place and environment*, vi (2003), S. 131–41.

[17] Peter Wessel Zapffe, *Barske glæder*, hrsg. v. Sigmund Kvaløy (Oslo, 1969); und Sigmund Kvaløy, „Peter Wessel Zapffe og verdien av utemmet natur", in: Guttorm Fløistad und Per Fredrik Christiansen (Hrsg.), P. W. Zapffe: *Dikt og drama* (Oslo, 1970), S. 252–65.

[18] Nils Faarlund, *Friluftsliv: Hva – hvorfor – hvordan* (Oslo, 1973), S. 11; und Nils Faarlund, „Hva mener vi med friluftsliv?", *Mestre fjellet*, xv (1973), S. 4–6.

[19] Arne Næss, „The Norwegian roots of deep ecology", in: Børge Dahle (Hrsg.), *Nature: The true home of culture* (Oslo, 1994), S. 15–19; Nils Faarlund, „Hva mener vi med friluftsliv?", in: *Mestre fjellet*, xv (1973), S. 4–6; ders., „Friluftsliv – A Way Home", in: Børge Dahle (Hrsg.), *Nature: The true home of culture* (Oslo, 1994), S. 21–26; und Sigmund Kvaløy Setereng, „Inside nature", *ibid.*, S. 29–37.

[20] Sigmund Kvaløy, *Musikk-kritikk og kommunikasjon* (Oslo, 1965); und Nils Faarlund, „Sigmund 70 år!", *Tindeposten*, iv (2004), S. 16–19.

[21] Max Weber, *Wissenschaft als Beruf*, a.a.O., S. 498.

[22] Eivind Østbye u.a., „Hardangervidda, Norway", in: *Ecological bulletins*, xx (1975), S. 225–64; und Eilif Dahl, „Globale ressursproblemer", in: *Samtiden*, lxxxii (1973), S. 257–67.

[23] Torstein Engelskjøn, *Biologisk forskning i Norge: En analyse med spesiell vekt på grunnforskningens ressurser, organisasjon og innhold* (Oslo, 1972), S. 7–8, S. 39–40.

[24] Ragnhild Sundby, „Globalforgiftning", in: *Naturen*, lxxxix (1965), S. 3–11; Rachel Carson, *Silent Spring* (Greenwich, 1962); und ders., *Den tause våren* (Oslo, 1962).

[25] Rolf Vik, „Hvor står biologene i teknikkens århundre?", in: *Naturen*, xci (1967), S. 259–69, hier S. 269; Georg Henrik von Wright, „Essay om naturen, mennesket og den vitenskaplig-tekniske revolusjon", in: *Naturen*, xci (1967), S. 155–80; Jaques Yves Cousteau, „Er klokken blitt tolv?", in: *Naturen*, xciv (1970), S. 411–20; Lynn White, „Den økologiske krises historiske røtter", in: *Naturen*, xcv (1971), S. 77–92; Brunjulf Valum (hrsg. und übs.), *Øko-katastrofe: Artikler fra det amerikanske tidsskrift Ramparts med to tillegg om Mardøla-saken* (Oslo, 1971); und Bjørn L. Hegseth, *Miljøkunnskap – miljøvern: Forsøk på en oversikt* (Trondheim, 1970).

[26] Chunglin Kwa, „Representations of nature

[38] Rasmus Lyngnes, "Kan biologisk kunnskap gjeve dei unge mål og meining med livet", in *Naturen*, xcvi (1972), pp. 392–8; and Norges Offentlige Utredninger, *Bruken av Hardangervidda* (Oslo, 1974).

[39] Ivar Mysterud (ed.), *Forurensning og biologisk miljøvern* (Oslo, 1971); Ivar Mysterud, *Noen økologiske grunnbegreper* (Oslo, 1973); and idem, "Endringer i miljø og fauna", in Ragnar Fris Lid and Arne Semb-Johanssen (eds), *Norske dyr* (Oslo, 1971), v, pp. 412–28.

[40] Ivar Mysterud, "En kommentar til økologisk forskning", *Forskningsnytt*, xiv (1969), pp. 18–25, see p. 24.

[41] Ivar Mysterud and Magnar Norderhaug, "Økopolitikk – naturvernets nye dimensjon", in *Norsk natur*, vii (1970), pp. 24–27, see p. 25.

[42] Birgit Wiggen, *Debatten omrking populisme/økopolitikk i Norge 1966–1976: Ei litteraturliste* (Oslo, 1976); Ottar Brox, *Hva skjer i Nord-Norge* (Oslo, 1966); and Hartivg Sætra, *Den økopolitiske sosialismen* (Oslo, 1973).

[43] Ivar Mysterud and Magnar Norderhaug, "Koblingen mellom økologi og politikk", in *Norsk natur*, viii (1972), pp. 6–11; Kenneth E. Boulding, "The economics of the coming spaceship Earth", in Henry Jarrett (ed.), *Environmental quality in a growing economy* (Baltimore, 1966), pp. 3–14; idem, *Beyond economics* (Ann Arbor, 1968); Herman E. Daly, "Toward a steady-state economy", in J. Harte and R. Socolow (eds), *The patient Earth* (New York, 1971), pp. 237–51; and idem (ed.), *Toward a steady-state economy* (San Francisco, 1973).

[44] Ivar Mysterud and Magnar Norderhaug, "Teknisk-økonomiske løsninger på den økologiske krise?", in *Norsk natur*, viii (1972), pp. 12–16; idem, "Et samfunn i likevekt", lecture at The Student Union, The Norwegian School of Technology, Trondheim, 15 April 1972, 13 pp., personal archive; and idem, "Mirakeløkonomi og vekstsyke i Japan", in *Norsk natur*, viii (1972), pp. 4–6.

[45] Nils Chr. Stenseth, "En oppfordring til biologene om å utforme en økopolitikk", in *Naturen*, xcvi (1972), pp. 118–26, see p. 118.

[46] Ivar Mysterud, "En kommentar til økologisk forskning", in *Forskningsnytt*, xiv (1969), pp. 18–25, see p. 25; Nils Chr. Stenseth, "Matematisk modellbygging i økologisk forskning", in *Forskningsnytt*, xix (1974), pp. 28–34; and idem, *Theoretical studies on fluctuating populations: An evolutionary approach* (Oslo, 1977).

[47] Arne Næss, "Forskerens ansvar i miljøkrisen", in *Forskningsnytt*, xvii (1972), pp. 48–51, see p. 48.

[48] Anonymous (ed.), *Og etter oss ...* (Oslo, 1970); anonymous, "Og etter oss", in *Norsk natur*, v (1969), pp. 34–39; Erling Amble and Henning Hansen, *Det kapitalistiske boligproblemet* (Oslo, 1970); and Erling Amble, *Avfallsbehandling og planlegging* (Oslo, 1973).

mediating between ecology and science policy: The case of the International Biological Programme", *Social studies of science*, xvii (1987), S. 413–42; und Edgar B. Worthington (Hrsg.), *The evolution of IBP* (Cambridge, 1975).

[27] Rolf Vik, *International Biological Programme: Final report Scandinavian countries* (Oslo, 1975), S. 7; International Biological Programme, *IBP i Norge: Årsrapport* (Oslo, 1968–74); und F. E. Wielgolaski, „Fenologi, produksjonsøkologi og andre kjente eller ukjente økologiske begreper", in: *Naturen*, xcii (1968), S. 179–84.

[28] Rolf Vik und F. E. Wielgolaski, „Det Internationale Biologiske Program i 1969", in: *Forskingsnytt*, xv (1970), S. 14–20, hier S. 14, 16.

[29] Knut Fægri, „Den klassiske biologis stilling i moderne naturvitenskap", in: *Naturen*, xc (1966), S. 528–46, hier S. 531, 540; und Nils Roll-Hansen, *Det Internasjonale Biologiske Program (IBP) i Norge* (Oslo, 1982).

[30] Rolf Vik, „Naturvern er menneksevern", in: *Naturen*, xc (1966), S. 195–205, hier S. 195; und ders., „Hvor står biologien I teknikkens århundre?", in: *Forskningsnytt*, xi (1966), S. 16–19.

[31] Eilif Dahl zitiert in: N.N. (Hrsg.), *Working meeting on analysis of ecosystems: Tundra zone* (Ustaoset, 1968), S. 7. Vgl. auch Arne Semb-Johansson, „Samspillet i naturen", in: Ragnar Frislid und Aren Semb-Johansson (Hrsg.), *Norges dyr* (Oslo, 1971), v, S. 44–58.

[32] N.N. (Hrsg.), *Working meeting* (ref. 31), S. 32.

[33] Olav Gjærevoll, „Forord", in: Nalle Valtiala, *Mennesket – et skadedyr?* (Oslo, 1970), S. 7–8.

[34] Anonymous, „‚Aksjon Hardangervidda' i gang", in: *Norsk natur*, vi (1970), S. 122–4; und Jan Økland, „Naturviten og naturbruk: Om dyreliv og miljøforhold I norske vassdrag", in: *Naturen*, xci (1967), S. 387–97.

[35] Olav R. Skage, *Hardangervidda: Naturvern – kraftutbygging* (Oslo, 1971), 9. Skage Zusammenfassung bislang unveröffentlichter Berichte von Arne Semb-Johnsson, A. Løvlie, K. Elgmor, Ivar Mysterud, und Eivind Østbye. Ivar Mysterud und Eivind Østbye, „Vitenskaplige interesser og vassdragsreguleringer på Hardangervidda", in: *Forsknignsnytt*, i (1972), S. 35–45; und ders., „The future of Hardangervidda", in: *Research in Norway*, i (1973), S. 57–68.

[36] Rolf Vik (Hrsg.), „Forord", in: *Vassdrag og samfunn*, (Oslo, 1971), S. 11; und ders., „Vårt miljø og biologenes ansvar", *Samtiden*, lxxviii (1969), S. 67–69.

[37] Hans Skjervheim, „Naturvern og politikk", Øyvind Østerud, „Naturverdier og samfunn – en ideologisk skisse"; und Gunnar Skirbekk, „Distrikshøgskolar, mot-ekspertise og populisme", in: *Vassdrag og samfunn*, Rolf Vik (Hrsg.), (Oslo, 1971), S. 180–8, S. 189–210, S. 213–34, hier S. 181; und Per S. Enger, „Hva nå med norsk biologi?", in: Nils Roll-Hansen und Hans Skoie (Hrsg.), *Forskningspolitiske spørsmål i norsk biologi* (Oslo, 1974), S. 86–96.

[38] Rasmus Lyngnes, „Kan biologisk kunnskap gjeve dei unge mål og meining med livet", in: *Naturen*, xcvi

[49] Rolf Vik, "Kjenner vi vårt miljø? – Tar vi vare på det?", in anonymous (ed.), *Fem på tolv: En bok av vitenskapsmenn om vår mulige fremtid* (Oslo, 1968), pp. 125–54; idem, "Trusselen mot miljøet", in anonymous (ed.), *Verden i dag* (Oslo, 1969), pp. 79–92; and Eilif Dahl, *Økologi for ingeniører og arkitekter* (Oslo, 1969).

[50] Per Fredrik Christiansen and Helge Vold, *Kampen om universitetet: Boken fra filosofistudentenes aksjonsuke* (Oslo, 1969). For early criticisms of Næss see, for example, Hans Skjervehim, *Deltakar og tilskodar* (Oslo, 1957); and Helge Høibraaten, "Norway in 1968 and its aftermath: Maoism, the power of the periphery and the cultural upper class of the sixty-eighters", in Guri Hjeltnes (ed.), *Universitetet og studentene* (Oslo, 1998), 184–91.

[51] Sigmund Kvaløy, "To økosofier i Norge: Deres begynnelse og en del til", *Norsk filosofisk tidsskrift*, xxxvii (2002), pp. 117–25, see p. 122.

[52] People active in the seminars between 1969 and 1972 included Finn Alnæs, Reidar Eriksen, Nils Faarlund, Per Garder, Jon Godal, Jon Grepstad, Hjalmar Hegge, Paul Hofseth, Oddmund Hollås, Karl Georg Høyer, Sigmund Kvaløy, Johan Marstrander, Ivar Mysterud, Arne Næss, Sven Erik Skønberg, Ragnhild Sletelid, Svein Smelvær, Erna Stene, Arne Vinje, Jon Wetlesen, and probably many more. See Sigmund Kvaløy Setereng, "Økokrise – glimt fra det norske økofilosofiske forsøket", in *Den uoverstigelige grense* (Oslo, 1991), pp. 102–16; and Finn Alnæs, *Svart snø eller samvern: Dokumentarbok fra en brytningstid* (Oslo, 1976).

[53] Nils Roll-Hansen, "Naturvern eller menneskevern?", *Dagbladet*, 20 April 1970; and idem, "Hva slags natur ønsker vi?", in *Samtiden*, lxxxii (1973), pp. 285–95.

[54] Sigmund Kvaløy, 30 Oct. 1969, quoted in Finn Alnæs, *Svart snø eller samvern* (Oslo, 1976), 1; Bredo Berntsen, "Radikal, liberal, konservativ – en grenseoppgang", in *Samtiden*, lxxxi (1972), pp. 178–85; Paul Hofseth, "Fra estetikk til økopolitikk", in Bredo Berntsen (ed.), *Fra blomsterfredning til økopolitikk: Østlandske Naturvernforening 1914–1974* (Oslo, 1975), pp. 44–50; and Frode Gundersen, "Utviklingstrekk ved miljøbevegelsen i Norge", *Sosiologi i dag*, ii (1991), pp. 12–35.

[55] Jon Grepstad (ed.), *Mardøla: Dokumentasjon og perspektiv* (Oslo, 1971), chap. 3, p. 24; Nils Petter Gleditsch, Åke Hartmann and Jon Naustalslid, *Mardøla-aksjonen* (Oslo, 1971); Sigmund Kvaløy, "Mardøla, miljøvern og maktspill", in Brunjulf Valum (ed.), *Øko-katastrofe* (Oslo, 1971), pp. 153–62; idem, "Mardøla, Masi: Vår egen tid", interview in Magnar Mikkelsen, *Masi, Norge* (Oslo, 1971), pp. 97–111; and Ketil Lehland, "Mardøla etc., især det siste", in *Samtiden*, lxxix (1970), pp. 517–22.

(1972), S. 392–8; und Norges Offentlige Utredninger, *Bruken av Hardangervidda* (Oslo, 1974).

39 Ivar Mysterud (Hrsg.), *Forurensning og biologisk miljøvern* (Oslo, 1971); Ivar Mysterud, *Noen økologiske grunnbegreper* (Oslo, 1973); und ders., „Endringer i miljø og fauna", in: Ragnar Fris Lid und Arne Semb-Johanssen (Hrsg.), *Norske dyr* (Oslo, 1971), v, S. 412–28.

40 Ivar Mysterud, „En kommentar til økologisk forskning", *Forskningsnytt*, xiv (1969), S. 18–25, hier S. 24.

41 Ivar Mysterud und Magnar Norderhaug, „Økopolitikk – naturvernets nye dimensjon", in: *Norsk natur*, vii (1970), S. 24–27, hier S. 25.

42 Birgit Wiggen, *Debatten omrking populisme/økopolitikk i Norge 1966–1976: Ei litteraturliste* (Oslo, 1976); Ottar Brox, *Hva skjer i Nord-Norge* (Oslo, 1966); und Hartivg Sætra, *Den økopolitiske sosialismen* (Oslo, 1973).

43 Ivar Mysterud und Magnar Norderhaug, „Koblingen mellom økologi og politikk", in: *Norsk natur*, viii (1972), S. 6–11; Kenneth E. Boulding, „The economics of the coming spaceship Earth", in: Henry Jarrett (Hrsg.), *Environmental quality in a growing economy* (Baltimore, 1966), S. 3–14; ders., *Beyond economics* (Ann Arbor, 1968); Herman E. Daly, „Toward a steady-state economy", in: J. Harte und R. Socolow (Hrsg.), *The patient Earth* (New York, 1971), S. 237–51; und ders. (Hrsg.), *Toward a steady-state economy* (San Francisco, 1973).

44 Ivar Mysterud und Magnar Norderhaug, „Teknisk-økonomiske løsninger på den økologiske krise?", in: *Norsk natur*, viii (1972), S. 12–16; ders., „Et samfunn i likevekt", Vortrag in The Student Union, The Norwegian School of Technology, Trondheim, 15. April 1972, 13 Seiten, Privatarchiv; und ders., „Mirakeløkonomi og vekstsyke i Japan", in: *Norsk natur*, viii (1972), S. 4–6.

45 Nils Chr. Stenseth, „En oppfordring til biologene om å utforme en økopolitikk", in: *Naturen*, xcvi (1972), S. 118–26, hier S. 118.

46 Ivar Mysterud, „En kommentar til økologisk forskning", in: *Forskningsnytt*, xiv (1969), S. 18–25, hier S. 25; Nils Chr. Stenseth, „Matematisk modellbygging i økologisk forskning", in: *Forskningsnytt*, xix (1974), S. 28–34; und ders., *Theoretical studies on fluctuating populations: An evolutionary approach* (Oslo, 1977).

47 Arne Næss, „Forskerens ansvar i miljøkrisen", in: *Forskningsnytt*, xvii (1972), S. 48–51, hier S. 48.

48 N.N. (Hrsg.), *Og etter oss ...* (Oslo, 1970); N.N., „Og etter oss", in: *Norsk natur*, v (1969), S. 34–39; Erling Amble und Henning Hansen, *Det kapitalistiske boligproblemet* (Oslo, 1970); und Erling Amble, *Avfallsbehandling og planlegging* (Oslo, 1973).

49 Rolf Vik, „Kjenner vi vårt miljø? – Tar vi vare på det?", in: N.N. (Hrsg.), *Fem på tolv: En bok av vitenskapsmenn om vår mulige fremtid* (Oslo, 1968), S. 125–54; ders., „Trusselen mot miljøet", in: N.N.

56 Karl Marx, "Theses on Feuerbach" (1888) in D. McLellan (ed.), *Karl Marx: Selected writings* (New York, 1977), pp. 158.

57 Næss, quoted in a debate with Alfred J. Ayer in Fons Folders (ed.), *Reflexive water: The basic concerns of mankind* (London, 1974), pp. 26.

58 Arne Næss, *Økologi og filosofi I* (Oslo, 1971), p. 54.

59 Næss, *Økologi og filosofi I* (ref. 58), 59; and Mao Tsetung, *Mao Tsetungs dikt*, transl. by Kjell Heggelund and Tor Obrestad (Oslo, 1971).

60 Arne Næss, *Mao Tsetung: Massene filosoferer* (Oslo, 1974); idem, *Filosofiens historie*, 6th edn, ii (Oslo, 1980); and Judith Shapiro, *Mao's war against nature: Politics and the environment in revolutionary China* (Cambridge, 2001).

61 Sigmund Kvaløy, "Økologi – vannkraft – samfunn", *Norsk natur*, vi (1970), pp. 150–62; Herbert Marcuse, *One dimensional man: Studies in the ideology of advanced industrial society* (London, 1964); and Hjalmar Hegge, "Økonomisk vekst eller økologisk likevekt", *Samtiden*, lxxxi (1972), pp. 74–81.

62 Sigmund Kvaløy, "Eikesdal-Grytten i naturvernåret – utbyggernes glansnummer", *Norsk natur*, vi (1970), 69; idem, "Mardøla, miljøvern og maktspel", *Senit*, iii (1970), pp. 4–11; idem, "Mardøla – samvær som kampform", *Mestre fjellet*, i (1971), pp. 5–13; and idem, "Mangfold er livsstyrke!", *Byggekunst*, liii (1971), pp. 126–8.

63 Sigmund Kvaløy, *Øko-filosofi: Litteraturliste og orientering til studenter og andre interesserte* (Oslo, 1971), p. 1.

64 On oriental ecological encounters see Stephen Howe, "When – if ever – did empire end? Recent studies of imperialism and decolonization", in *Journal of contemporary history*, xl (2005), pp. 585–99; J. M. Powell, "The empire meets the new deal: Interwar encounters in conservation and regional planning", in *Geographical research*, xliii (2005), pp. 337–60; Jane Carruthers, "Africa: Histories, ecologies and societies", in *Environment and history*, x (2004), pp. 379–406; Stephen Bocking, "Empires of ecology", in *Studies in history and philosophy of biological and biomedical sciences*, xxxv (2004), pp. 793–801; and Richard Grove, *Green imperialism: Colonial expansion, tropical island Edens and the origins of environmentalism* (Cambridge, 1995).

65 Anonymous (ed.), *Tirich Mir: The Norwegian Himalaya expedition* (London, 1952); and Per Wendelbo, "Plants from Tirich Mir: A contribution to the flora of Hindukush", in *Nytt magasin for botanikk*, i (1952), pp. 1–70. This article became Wendelbo's M.A. thesis in systematic botany at the University of Oslo in 1953. Wendelbo became a leading botanist of Iranian plants and a professor at Gothenburg University.

66 The 'T' could also be short for Tvergastein, the name of Næss's cottage near Finse, or also "tolkning"

(Hrsg.), *Verden i dag* (Oslo, 1969), S. 79–92; und Eilif Dahl, *Økologi for ingeniører og arkitekter* (Oslo, 1969).

50 Per Fredrik Christiansen und Helge Vold, *Kampen om universitetet: Boken fra filosofistudentenes aksjonsuke* (Oslo, 1969). Zu frühen kritischen Schriften zu Næss siehe beispielsweise Hans Skjervehim, *Deltakar og tilskodar* (Oslo, 1957); und Helge Høibraaten, „Norway in 1968 and its aftermath: Maoism, the power of the periphery and the cultural upper class of the sixty-eighters", in: Guri Hjeltnes (Hrsg.), *Universitetet og studentene* (Oslo, 1998), 184–91.

51 Sigmund Kvaløy, „To økosofier i Norge: Deres begynnelse og en del til", *Norsk filosofisk tidsskrift*, xxxvii (2002), S. 117–25, hier S. 122.

52 Zwischen 1969 und 1972 in den Seminaren aktiv waren Finn Alnæs, Reidar Eriksen, Nils Faarlund, Per Garder, Jon Godal, Jon Grepstad, Hjalmar Hegge, Paul Hofseth, Oddmund Hollås, Karl Georg Høyer, Sigmund Kvaløy, Johan Marstrander, Ivar Mysterud, Arne Næss, Sven Erik Skønberg, Ragnhild Sletelid, Svein Smelvær, Erna Stene, Arne Vinje, Jon Wetlesen und wahrscheinlich viele weitere. Siehe Sigmund Kvaløy Setereng, „Økokrise – glimt fra det norske økofilosofiske forsøket", in: *Den uoverstigelige grense* (Oslo, 1991), S. 102–16; und Finn Alnæs, *Svart snø eller samvern: Dokumentarbok fra en brytningstid* (Oslo, 1976).

53 Nils Roll-Hansen, „Naturvern eller menneskevern?", *Dagbladet*, 20 April 1970; und ders., „Hva slags natur ønsker vi?", in: *Samtiden*, lxxxii (1973), S. 285–95.

54 Sigmund Kvaløy, 30 Oct. 1969, zitiert in: Finn Alnæs, *Svart snø eller samvern* (Oslo, 1976), 1; Bredo Berntsen, „Radikal, liberal, konservativ – en grenseoppgang", in: *Samtiden*, lxxxi (1972), S. 178–85; Paul Hofseth, „Fra estetikk til økopolitikk", in: Bredo Berntsen (Hrsg.), *Fra blomsterfredning til økopolitikk: Østlandske Naturvernforening 1914–1974* (Oslo, 1975), S. 44–50; und Frode Gundersen, „Utviklingstrekk ved miljøbevegelsen i Norge", *Sosiologi i dag*, ii (1991), S. 12–35.

55 Jon Grepstad (Hrsg.), *Mardøla: Dokumentasjon og perspektiv* (Oslo, 1971), Kap. 3, S. 24; Nils Petter Gleditsch, Åke Hartmann und Jon Naustalslid, *Mardøla-aksjonen* (Oslo, 1971); Sigmund Kvaløy, „Mardøla, miljøvern og maktspill", in: Brunjulf Valum (Hrsg.), *Øko-katastrofe* (Oslo, 1971), S. 153–62; ders., „Mardøla, Masi: Vår egen tid", Interview mit Magnar Mikkelsen, *Masi, Norge* (Oslo, 1971), S. 97–111; und Ketil Lehland, „Mardøla etc., især det siste", in: *Samtiden*, lxxix (1970), S. 517–22.

56 Karl Marx, Thesen über Feuerbach, MEW 3:7 (These 11), Karl Marx: *Selected writings* (New York, 1977), S. 158.

57 Næss, zitiert nach einer Diskussion mit Alfred J. Ayer in: Fons Folders (Hrsg.), *Reflexive water: The basic concerns of mankind* (London, 1974), S. 26.

58 Arne Næss, *Økologi og filosofi I* (Oslo, 1971), S. 54.

59 Næss, *Økologi og filosofi I* (ref. 58), 59; und Mao

(interpretation) as this was important to Næss's early philosophy. There is, however, only circumstantial evidence for these readings. Arne Næss, *Opp stupet til østtoppen av Tirich Mir* (Oslo, 1964), p. 126; idem, *Økologi, samfunn og livsstil*, 5th edn (Oslo, 1976), p. 78; and Geir Grimeland, *En historie om klatring I Norge: 1900–2000* (Oslo, 2004), pp. 75–81.

67 Johan Galtung and Arne Næss, *Gandhis politiske etikk* (Oslo, 1955); Arne Næss, "Gandhis lære og situasjonen i dag", in *Forskningsnytt*, v (1960), pp. 2–4; and idem, *Gandhi og atomalderen* (Oslo, 1960).

68 Arne Næss, *Gandhi and the Nuclear Age* (New Jersey, 1965); P. F. Power, "Gandhi and the Nuclear Age", *Annals of American academics*, ccclxviii (1967), p. 201; Mulford Q. Sibley, "Gandhi and the Nuclear Age", *Political science quarterly*, lxxxii (1967), pp. 144–5; D. Dalton, "Gandhi and the Nuclear Age", *Political studies*, xv (1967), pp. 251–2; anonymous, "Gandhi and the nuclear age", *Choice*, iii (1967), p. 364; Lore L. Kopp, "Gandhi and the Nuclear Age", *Kyklos*, xix (1966), pp. 764–5; and H. Arthur Steiner, "Gandhi and the nuclear age", *Western political quarterly*, xix (1966), pp. 547–8. For a review of reviews of Næss's books see Peder Anker, "Arne Næss sett utenfra", *Samtiden*, iv (2002), pp. 4–19.

69 Kvaløy, "To økosofier i Norge: Deres begynnelse og en del til" (ref. 51).

70 Sigmund Kvaløy, "Forord", in Stein Jarving (ed.), *Likevektssamfunn* (Karlsøy, 1976), pp. 6–7.

71 Sigmund Kvaløy, "Likevektssamfunnet: Sherpasamfunnet i Rolwaling", *Aftenposten A-magasin*, 1972, 7–9, reprinted in Sigmund Kvaløy, *Økokrise, natur og menneske* (Oslo, 1973), pp. 65–88, see pp. 65, 86.

72 Torbjørn Ydegaard, *Sherpa – folket under Everest* (Holte, 1988), p. 20.

73 Erling Dekke Næss, *Autobiography of a shipping man* (Colchester, 1977), pp. 252–4; and Kvaløy, "Likevektssamfunnet" (ref. 70), p. 67.

74 Kvaløy, "Likevektssamfunnet" (ref. 70), pp. 65, 75.

75 Sigmund Kvaløy, "Rolwaling – et livssamfunn i likevekt", in *Mestre fjellet*, xv (1973), pp. 11–12.

76 Nils Faarlund, "Hvorfor", *Mestre fjellet*, xiii (1972), pp. 6–7, see p. 6; and idem, "Bidrag til en ekspedisjonssosiologi", in *Mestre fjellet*, xiii (1972), pp. 11–14.

77 Næss, *Økologi, samfunn og livsstil* (ref. 66), p. 309; and idem, "Mountains", in *The trumpeter*, xxi (2005), pp. 51–54.

78 Arne Næss, "Blodigle og menneske", *Mestre fjellet*, xiii (1972), p. 18.

79 Arne Næss, "Skytsgudinnen Gauri Shankar: Apell om fredning", in *Mestre fjellet*, xiii (1972), p. 15; and Nils Faarlund, *Glimt fra klatringen på eggen*, ibid., pp. 9–10.

Tsetung, *Mao Tsetungs dikt*, übs. von Kjell Heggelund und Tor Obrestad (Oslo, 1971).

[60] Arne Næss, *Mao Tsetung: Massene filosoferer* (Oslo, 1974); ders., *Filosofiens historie*, 6th edn, ii (Oslo, 1980); und Judith Shapiro, *Mao's war against nature: Politics and the environment in revolutionary China* (Cambridge, 2001).

[61] Sigmund Kvaløy, „Økologi – vannkraft – samfunn", *Norsk natur*, vi (1970), S. 150–62; Herbert Marcuse, *One dimensional man: Studies in the ideology of advanced industrial society* (London, 1964); und Hjalmar Hegge, „Økonomisk vekst eller økologisk likevekt", *Samtiden*, lxxxi (1972), S. 74–81.

[62] Sigmund Kvaløy, „Eikesdal-Grytten i naturvernåret – utbyggernes glansnummer", *Norsk natur*, vi (1970), 69; ders., „Mardøla, miljøvern og maktspel", *Senit*, iii (1970), S. 4–11; ders., „Mardøla – samvær som kampform", *Mestre fjellet*, i (1971), S. 5–13; und ders., „Mangfold er livsstyrke!", *Byggekunst*, liii (1971), S. 126–8.

[63] Sigmund Kvaløy, *Øko-filosofi: Litteraturliste og orientering til studenter og andre interesserte* (Oslo, 1971), S. 1.

[64] Zu fernöstlichen ökologischen Begegnungen siehe Stephen Howe, „When – if ever – did empire end? Recent studies of imperialism and decolonization", in: *Journal of contemporary history*, xl (2005), S. 585–99; J. M. Powell, „The empire meets the new deal: Interwar encounters in conservation and regional planning", in: *Geographical research*, xliii (2005), S. 337–60; Jane Carruthers, „Africa: Histories, ecologies and societies", in: *Environment and history*, x (2004), S. 379–406; Stephen Bocking, „Empires of ecology", in: *Studies in history and philosophy of biological and biomedical sciences*, xxxv (2004), S. 793–801; und Richard Grove, *Green imperialism: Colonial expansion, tropical island Edens and the origins of environmentalism* (Cambridge, 1995).

[65] N.N. (Hrsg.), *Tirich Mir: The Norwegian Himalaya expedition* (London, 1952); und Per Wendelbo, „Plants from Tirich Mir: A contribution to the flora of Hindukush", in: *Nytt magasin for botanikk*, i (1952), S. 1–70. Aus diesem Artikel erwuchs Wendelbos Magisterarbeit in systematischer Biologie an der Universität Oslo 1953. Wendelbo wurde zu einem führenden Botaniker auf dem Gebiet iranischer Pflanzen und übernahm eine Professur an der Universität Gothenburg.

[66] Das »T« könnte auch für Tvergastein stehen, wie Næss sein Häuschen bei Finse nannte, oder für »tolkning« (Deutung), die in Næss' früher Philosophie eine wichtige Rolle spielte. Allerdings gibt es für diese Lesarten nur einen Beleg. Arne Næss, *Opp stupet til østtoppen av Tirich Mir* (Oslo, 1964), S. 126; ders., *Økologi, samfunn og livsstil*, 5th edn (Oslo, 1976), S. 78; und Geir Grimeland, *En historie om klatring I Norge: 1900–2000* (Oslo, 2004), S. 75–81.

[67] Johan Galtung und Arne Næss, *Gandhis politiske*

[80] See, for example, Arne Næss Jr, *Drangnag-Ri: Det hellige fjellet* (Oslo, 1995).

[81] Sigmund Kvaløy, "Norwegian ecophilosophy and ecopolitics and their influence from Buddhism", in Klas Sandell (ed.), *Buddhist perspectives on the ecocrisis* (Kandy, 1987), pp. 49–72.

[82] David R. Klein, *The emerging ecophilosophy*, 1972, unpublished typescript, 7pp., p. 4. I am grateful to Prof. Klein for making this manuscript available.

[83] Nils Faarlund, "Om økoliv", *Mestre fjellet*, xv (1973), pp. 7–9, see pp. 7, 8; idem, "Friluftsliv i barneog ungdomsskolen", *Vår skole*, lxi (1975), pp. 196–209; and Jon Skjeseth, *Mennesket og biosfæren: Biologi for gymnasets grunnkurs* (Oslo, 1972).

[84] Sigmund Kvaløy, *Øko-filosofisk fragment: Kompleksitet og komplikasjon* (Oslo, 1972).

[85] Sigmund Kvaløy, *Økokrise, natur og menneske* (Oslo, 1973), p. 131. Similarly in Richard Merrill (ed.), *Radical agriculture* (New York, 1976).

[86] Kvaløy, *Økokrise, natur og menneske* (ref. 85), p. 135

[87] Sigmund Kvaløy, "Ecophilosophy and ecopolitics: Thinking and acting in response to the threats of ecocatastrophe", *The North American review*, cclix (1974), pp. 16–28, see p. 24.

[88] Arne Næss, *Økologi og filosofi: Et økosofisk arbeidsutkast*, 3rd preliminary edn (Oslo, 1972), p. 7.

[89] Næss, *Økologi og filosofi* (ref. 88), 177.

[90] Jørgen Randers, *En undersøkelse av spinnsystemet i α-Fe_2O_3 ved uelastisk neutronspredning* (Kjeller, 1969); Donella H. Meadows, Dennis L. Meadows, Jørgen Randers and William W. Behrens III, *The limits to growth: A report for the Club of Rome's project on the predicament of mankind* (New York, 1972); and Jørgen Randers, *Conceptualizing dynamic models of social systems: Lessons from a study of social change* (Cambridge, 1973), 107–20.

[91] Wade Rowland, *The plot to save the world: The life and times of the Stockholm conference on the human environment* (Toronto, 1973), pp. 9–25; United Nations, *Report of the United Nations conference on the human environment* (New York, 1973); Charles T. Rubin, *The green crusade* (New York, 1994), pp. 130–41; and Arne Semb-Johansson, "Stockholm-konferansen kan få stor betydning", *Forskningsnytt*, xvii (1972), pp. 7–10

[92] John McHale, "Future research: Some integrative and communicative aspects", in Robert Jungk and Johan Galtung (eds), *Mankind 2000* (Oslo, 1970); idem, *The future of the future* (New York, 1969); idem, *The ecological context* (New York, 1970); and Richard Buckminster Fuller, *Operating manual for spaceship Earth* (Edwardsville, 1969).

[93] Licinius Ciplea, "The technological parameters of long range ecological politics" (abstract), in *3rd World future research conference: Abstracts*, ed. by Helen Seidler and Cristina Krikorian (Bucharest, 1972), pp. 21–22; and Pavel Apostol, "English summary", *Calitatea vietii*

etikk (Oslo, 1955); Arne Næss, „Gandhis lære og situasjonen i dag", in: *Forskningsnytt*, v (1960), S. 2–4; und ders., *Gandhi og atomalderen* (Oslo, 1960).

[68] Arne Næss, *Gandhi and the Nuclear Age* (New Jersey, 1965); P. F. Power, „Gandhi and the Nuclear Age", *Annals of American academics*, ccclxviii (1967), S. 201; Mulford Q. Sibley, „Gandhi and the Nuclear Age", *Political science quarterly*, lxxxii (1967), S. 144–5; D. Dalton, „Gandhi and the Nuclear Age", *Political studies*, xv (1967), S. 251–2; N.N., „Gandhi and the nuclear age", *Choice*, iii (1967), S. 364; Lore L. Kopp, „Gandhi and the Nuclear Age", *Kyklos*, xix (1966), S. 764–5; und H. Arthur Steiner, „Gandhi and the nuclear age", *Western political quarterly*, xix (1966), S. 547–8. Eine Übersicht der Besprechungen zu Naess' Büchern siehe Peder Anker, „Arne Næss sett utenfra", *Samtiden*, iv (2002), S. 4–19.

[69] Kvaløy, „To økosofier i Norge: Deres begynnelse og en del til" (ref. 51).

[70] Sigmund Kvaløy, „Forord", in: Stein Jarving (Hrsg.), *Likevektssamfunn* (Karlsøy, 1976), S. 6–7.

[71] Sigmund Kvaløy, „Likevektssamfunnet: Sherpasamfunnet i Rolwaling", *Aftenposten A-magasin*, 1972, S. 7–9, wiederabgedruckt in: Sigmund Kvaløy, *Økokrise, natur og menneske* (Oslo, 1973), S. 65–88, hier S. 65, 86.

[72] Torbjørn Ydegaard, *Sherpa – folket under Everest* (Holte, 1988), S. 20.

[73] Erling Dekke Næss, *Autobiography of a shipping man* (Colchester, 1977), S. 252–4; und Kvaløy, „Likevektssamfunnet" (ref. 70), S. 67.

[74] Kvaløy, „Likevektssamfunnet" (ref. 70), S. 65, 75.

[75] Sigmund Kvaløy, „Rolwaling – et livssamfunn i likevekt", in: *Mestre fjellet*, xv (1973), S. 11–12.

[76] Nils Faarlund, „Hvorfor", *Mestre fjellet*, xiii (1972), S. 6–7, hier S. 6; und ders., „Bidrag til en ekspedisjonssosiologi", in: *Mestre fjellet*, xiii (1972), S. 11–14.

[77] Næss, *Økologi, samfunn og livsstil* (ref. 66), S. 309; und ders., „Mountains", in: *The trumpeter*, xxi (2005), S. 51–54.

[78] Arne Næss, „Blodigle og menneske", *Mestre fjellet*, xiii (1972), S. 18.

[79] Arne Næss, „Skytsgudinnen Gauri Shankar: Apell om fredning", in: *Mestre fjellet*, xiii (1972), S. 15; und Nils Faarlund, *Glimt fra klatringen på eggen*, ders., S. 9–10.

[80] Siehe beispielsweise Arne Næss Jr, *Drangnag-Ri: Det hellige fjellet* (Oslo, 1995).

[81] Sigmund Kvaløy, „Norwegian ecophilosophy and ecopolitics and their influence from Buddhism", in: Klas Sandell (Hrsg.), *Buddhist perspectives on the ecocrisis* (Kandy, 1987), S. 49–72.

[82] David R. Klein, *The emerging ecophilosophy*, 1972, unveröffentlichtes Typoskript, 7 Seiten, S. 4. Ich danke Prof. Klein, der mir dieses Manuskript zu Verfügung gestellt hat.

[83] Nils Faarlund, „Om økoliv", *Mestre fjellet*, xv (1973),

si explorarea viitorului (Bucharest, 1975), pp. 258–69.

[94] Johan Galtung, *Kologi og klassepolitik* (Copenhagen, 1972), 12, 14, 22 (shorter version published as "Økologi og klassekamp", *Samtiden*, lxxxii (1973), pp. 65–83; and Johan Galtung and Fumiko Nishimura, *Kan vi lære av Kineserne?* (Oslo, 1975).

[95] Jim Dator, "The WFSF and I", in *Futures*, xxxvii (2005), pp. 371–85, see p. 373; G. F., "Third World future research conference", *Futures*, iv (1972), pp. 381–2; Irving H. Buchen, "Futuristic conference in Romania", in *The futurist*, vii (1973), pp. 31–32; and Bart van Steenbergen, "The first fifteen years: A personal view of the early history of the WFSF", in *Futures*, xxxvii (2005), pp. 355–60.

[96] Nicolae Ceauşescu, "Opening remarks", in "Management science and futures studies in socialist Romania", in *Viitorul social*, special issue (Bucharest, 1972), pp. 7–18.

[97] To my knowledge, the original lecture exists only in Romanian as Arne Næss, "Miscarea eclogică superficială si profundă", in *Viitorul comun al oamenilor: Comunicări prezentate la cea de-a III-a Conferință mondială de cercetare a viitorului, Bucuresti, Septembrie 1972*, ed. by Mihai Botez and Mircea Ioanid (Bucharest, 1976), pp. 275–83, see pp. 275, 276, 278. I am grateful to Erling Schller for a translation of this document. A summary of the lecture was published by Næss as "The shallow and the deep, long-range ecology movements: A summary", in *Inquiry*, xvi (1973), pp. 95–100.

[98] Næss, *Miscarea ecologică superficială si profundă* (ref. 97), p. 281.

[99] Grimeland, *En historie om klatring* (ref. 66), p. 122; Jardar Seim, "Miljøvern utan politiske følgjer?", *Syn og segn*, lxxviii (1972), pp. 515–24; and anonymous [attributed to Samarbeidsgruppa for natur og miljøvern], *Håndbok i miljøvern: Økopolitisk strategi og taktikk* (Oslo, 1973).

[100] Samarbeidsgruppa for natur og miljøvern, *Dette bør du vite om EF* (Oslo, 1972), p. 91; and Tor Bjørklund, *Mot strømmen: Kampen mot EF 1961–1972* (Oslo, 1982).

[101] Ivar Mystrud, "Økopolitikk, biologi og klassekamp", in *Norsk natur*, vii (1971), pp. 123–7; Bjørn Unneberg, *Grønn sosialisme for utkantproletarer* (Oslo, 1971); Arne Semb-Johansson, Jon Lund Hansen and Ivar Mysterud, *Bred økologi: En tverrfaglig utfordring* (Oslo, 1993); and Ivar Mysterud and Iver Mysterud, "Reviving the ghost of broad ecology", in *Journal of social and evolutionary systems*, xvii (1994), pp. 167–95.

[102] Ragnar Frislid, Paul Hofseth and Johan Støyva (eds), *Miljøleksikon: Økologi, natur og miljøvern* (Oslo, 1976); Paul Hofseth (ed.), *Økofilosofisk lesebok* (2 vols, Oslo, 1974); Paul Hofseth and Arne Vinje (eds), *Økologi økofilosofi* (Oslo, 1975); and Reidar Eriksen, Per Halvorsen and Steve I. Johansen, *Aluminiums-*

S. 7–9, hier S. 7, 8; ders., „Friluftsliv i barneog ungdomsskolen", Vår skole, lxi (1975), S. 196–209; und Jon Skjeseth, Mennesket og biosfæren: Biologi for gymnasets grunnkurs (Oslo, 1972).

84 Sigmund Kvaløy, Øko-filosofisk fragment: Kompleksitet og komplikasjon (Oslo, 1972).

85 Sigmund Kvaløy, Økokrise, natur og menneske (Oslo, 1973), S. 131. Vgl. auch Richard Merrill (Hrsg.), Radical agriculture (New York, 1976).

86 Kvaløy, Økokrise, natur og menneske (ref. 85), S. 135

87 Sigmund Kvaløy, „Ecophilosophy and ecopolitics: Thinking and acting in response to the threats of ecocatastrophe", in: The North American review, cclix (1974), S. 16–28, hier S. 24.

88 Arne Næss, Økologi og filosofi: Et økosofisk arbeidsutkast, 3rd preliminary edn (Oslo, 1972), S. 7.

89 Næss, Økologi og filosofi (ref. 88), S. 177.

90 Jørgen Randers, En undersøkelse av spinnsystemet i α-Fe_2O_3 ved uelastisk neutronspredning (Kjeller, 1969); Donella H. Meadows, Dennis L. Meadows, Jrgen Randers und William W. Behrens III, The limits to growth: A report for the Club of Rome's project on the predicament of mankind (New York, 1972); und Jørgen Randers, Conceptualizing dynamic models of social systems: Lessons from a study of social change (Cambridge, 1973), S. 107–20.

91 Wade Rowland, The plot to save the world: The life and times of the Stockholm conference on the human environment (Toronto, 1973), S. 9–25; United Nations, Report of the United Nations conference on the human environment (New York, 1973); Charles T. Rubin, The green crusade (New York, 1994), S. 130–41; und Arne Semb-Johansson, „Stockholm-konferansen kan få stor betydning", Forskningsnytt, xvii (1972), S. 7–10

92 John McHale, in: „Future research: Some integrative and communicative aspects", in: Robert Jungk and Johan Galtung (Hrsg.), Mankind 2000 (Oslo, 1970); ders., The future of the future (New York, 1969); ders., The ecological context (New York, 1970); Richard Buckminster Fuller, Bedienungsanleitung für das Raumschiff Erde, Philo Fine Arts (Fundus Bd. 137), 1998.

93 Licinius Ciplea, „The technological parameters of long range ecological politics" (Auszug), in: 3rd World future research conference: Abstracts, hrsg. von Helen Seidler und Cristina Krikorian (Bukarest, 1972), S. 21–22; und Pavel Apostol, „English summary", Calitatea vietii si explorarea viitorului (Bukarest, 1975), S. 258–69.

94 Johan Galtung, Kologi og klassepolitik (Copenhagen, 1972), 12, 14, 22 (eine kürzere Fassung wurde veröffentlicht unter: „Økologi og klassekamp", Samtiden, lxxxii (1973), S. 65–83; und Johan Galtung und Fumiko Nishimura, Kan vi lære av Kineserne? (Oslo, 1975).

95 Jim Dator, "The WFSF and I", in: Futures, xxxvii (2005), S. 371–85, hier S. 373; G. F., „Third World future re search conference", Futures, iv (1972), S. 381–2; Irving H. Buchen, „Futuristic conference in Romania",

industriens framtid (Trondheim, 1977).

103 Stein Jarving, Grønt liv: En bok om alternativt jordbruk og et program for en bedre livsstandard (Oslo, 1974), p. 17; idem, Likevektssamfunn (ref. 70); Anders Lindhjem-Godal, "'Kjernefamilien er en sosial sjukdom': Kollektivliv på Karlsøy i Troms", in Tor Egil Frøland and Trine Rogg Korsvik (eds), 1968: Opprør og motkultur på norsk (Oslo, 2006), pp. 93–118.

104 Hartvig Sætra, Jamvektssamfunnet er ikkje noko urtete-selskap (Oslo, 1990); Lars Martin Hjorthol, Alta: Kraftkampen som utfordret statens makt (Oslo, 2006).

105 Gro Harlem Brundtland, Mitt liv: 1939–1986 (Oslo, 1997), pp. 125–50; idem, Tiltak for å hindre forurensning av våre store innsjøer (Trondheim, 1977); and World Commission on Environment and Development, Our Common Future (Oxford, 1987).

106 Arne Næss, "The shallow and the deep, long-range ecology movements: A summary", in Andrew Brennan and Nina Witoszek (eds), Philosophical dialogues (Boston, 1999), p. 7, note.

in: *The futurist*, vii (1973), S. 31–32; und Bart van Steenbergen, „The first fifteen years: A personal view of the early history of the WFSF", in: *Futures*, xxxvii (2005), S. 355–60.

[96] Nicolae Ceauşescu, „Opening remarks", in: „Management science and futures studies in socialist Romania", in: *Viitorul social*, Sonderausgabe (Bukarest, 1972), S. 7–18.

[97] Nach meiner Kenntnis liegt der Originalvortrag nur auf Rumänisch vor: Arne Næss, „Miscarea ecolgică superficială si profundă", in: *Viitorul comun al oamenilor: Comunicări prezentate la cea de-a III-a Conferintă mondială de cercetare a viitorului, Bucuresti, Septembrie 1972*, hrsg. von Mihai Botez und Mircea Ioanid (Bukarest, 1976), S. 275–83, hier S. 275, 276, 278. Ich danke Erling Schller für die Übersetzung dieses Dokuments. Eine Zusammenfassung seiner Rede veröffentlichte Næss unter dem Titel „The shallow and the deep, long-range ecology movements: A summary", in: *Inquiry*, xvi (1973), S. 95–100.

[98] Næss, *Miscarea ecolgică superficială si profundă* (ref. 97), S. 281.

[99] Grimeland, *En historie om klatring* (ref. 66), S. 122; Jardar Seim, „Miljøvern utan politiske følgjer?", *Syn og segn*, lxxviii (1972), S. 515–24; und N.N. [attributed to Samarbeidsgruppa for natur og miljøvern], *Håndbok i miljøvern: Økopolitisk strategi og taktikk* (Oslo, 1973).

[100] Samarbeidsgruppa for natur og miljøvern, *Dette bør du vite om EF* (Oslo, 1972), S. 91; und Tor Bjørklund, *Mot strømmen: Kampen mot EF 1961–1972* (Oslo, 1982).

[101] Ivar Mystrud, „Økopolitikk, biologi og klassekamp", in: *Norsk natur*, vii (1971), S. 123–7; Bjørn Unneberg, *Grønn sosialisme for utkantproletarer* (Oslo, 1971); Arne Semb-Johansson, Jon Lund Hansen und Ivar Mysterud, *Bred økologi: En tverrfaglig utfordring* (Oslo, 1993); und Ivar Mysterud und Iver Mysterud, „Reviving the ghost of broad ecology", in: *Journal of social and evolutionary systems*, xvii (1994), S. 167–95.

[102] Ragnar Frislid, Paul Hofseth und Johan Støyva (Hrsg.), *Miljøleksikon: Økologi, naturog miljøvern* (Oslo, 1976); Paul Hofseth (Hrsg.), *Økofilosofisk lesebok* (2 Bd., Oslo, 1974); Paul Hofseth und Arne Vinje (Hrsg.), *Økologi økofilosofi* (Oslo, 1975); und Reidar Eriksen, Per Halvorsen und Steve I. Johansen, *Aluminiumsindustriens framtid* (Trondheim, 1977).

[103] Stein Jarving, *Grønt liv: En bok om alternativt jordbruk og et program for en bedre livsstandard* (Oslo, 1974), S. 17; ders., *Likevektssamfunn* (ref. 70); Anders Lindhjem-Godal, „‚Kjernefamilien er en sosial sjukdom': Kollektivliv på Karlsøy i Troms", in: Tor Egil Frøland und Trine Rogg Korsvik (Hrsg.), *1968: Opprør og motkultur på norsk* (Oslo, 2006), S. 93–118.

[104] Hartvig Sætra, *Jamvektssamfunnet er ikkje noko urtete-selskap* (Oslo, 1990); Lars Martin Hjorthol, *Alta: Kraftkampen som utfordret statens makt*

(Oslo, 2006).

[105] Gro Harlem Brundtland, *Mitt liv: 1939–1986* (Oslo, 1997), S. 125–50; ders., *Tiltak for å hindre forurensning av våre store innsjøer* (Trondheim, 1977); und World Commission on Environment and Development, *Our Common Future* (Oxford, 1987).

[106] Arne Næss, „The shallow and the deep, long-range ecology movements: A summary", in: Andrew Brennan und Nina Witoszek (Hrsg.), *Philosophical dialogues* (Boston, 1999), S. 7, Anm.

Tue Greenfort

Lebt und arbeitet seit 2003 in Dänemark und Berlin
2000–2003 Studium an der Städelschule,
Frankfurt am Main bei Prof. Thomas Bayrle
1997–2000 Studium an der Akademie Fünen,
Dänemark bei Prof. Jesper Christiansen und
Prof. Lars Bent Petersen
1973 Geboren in Holbæk, Dänemark

Has since 2003 lived and worked in Denmark and Berlin.
2000–2003 studied at the Städel School in Frankfurt am
Main under Prof. Thomas Bayrle
1997–2000 studied at the Academy Fünen, Denmark
under Prof. Jesper Christiansen and Prof. Lars Bent
Petersen
1973 born in Holbæk, Denmark

Einzelausstellungen / Solo exhibitions

2012 Kunstraum Dornbirn, *Eine Berggeschichte*
The Feeder Canal Sand Martin Colony,
Permanente Installation im öffentlichen
Raum, Bristol, UK
2011 *NEOBIOTA*, Permanente Installation im
öffentlichen Raum, KVB Nord-Süd
Stadtbahn, U-Bahn Haltestelle Breslauer Platz,
Köln, Deutschland
Where the People Will Go, South London
Gallery, London, UK
2010 *Flambant Neuf*, Johann König, Berlin
2008 *Frieze Projects*, London, UK
Linear Deflection, Kunstverein Braunschweig
The Foundation, Fondazione Morra Greco,
Neapel, Italien
2007 Johann König, Berlin
Medusa, Secession, Wien, Österreich
Glucksman Gallery, Cork, Irland
2006 Max Wigram Gallery, London, UK
Photosynthesis, Witte de With, Rotterdam, NL
2005 *Betreten des Grundstücks erlaubt*,
Kunstverein Arnsberg
Als ob wir nicht die Besitzende wären,
Palais für aktuelle Kunst, Glückstadt
Dänische Schweine und andere Märkte,
Johann König, Berlin
2004 *Umwelt*, Gallery Zero, Mailand, Italien
Re Präsentation, 1822 Forum, Frankfurt am Main
Spediteur Zimmer, Galerie Nicolas Krupp,
Basel, Schweiz
2003 *Used and Produced*, Schnittraum, Köln
Fresh and Upcoming, Frankfurter Kunstverein,
Frankfurt am Main
2002 *Out of site*, Johann König, Berlin
2001 *The Peripheral Centre*, Dont-miss,
Frankfurt am Main
2000 *Exchange*, Elmgreen & Dragset in Zusammenarbeit mit NIFCA, Helsinki
Städelschule, Frankfurt am Main
1999 *Natur*, DFKU, Odense, Dänemark

**Gruppenausstellungen (Auswahl) /
Group shows (Selection)**

2012 dOCUMENTA(13), *The Worldly House*,
Co-Kurator, Kassel, Germany
Higher Atlas, Arts in Marrakech 4th Biennale,
Marrakech, Marokko
2011 *20 Jahre MMK*, Museum für Moderne Kunst, Frankfurt
Based in Berlin, Atelierhaus Monbijou Park, Berlin
Über die Metapher des Wachstums, Kunstverein
Hannover, Kunstverein Frankfurt,
Kunsthaus Baselland
Struktur & Organismus, kuratiert von
art:phalanx, Wachau, Österreich
2010 *Alter Natur*, Z33, Belgien
Freeze, Nils Stærk Galerie, Kopenhagen, Dänemark
Zur Nachahmung empfohlen!, Uferhallen Berlin
RESIDUAL, Goethe Institut, Mexiko Stadt, Mexiko
The woods that see and hear, Den Bosch, Niederlande
Power Games, Museum Ludwig, Budapest, Ungarn
Dopplereffekt. Bilder in Kunst und Wissenschaft,
Kunsthalle zu Kiel
Rethink Kakotopia, Tensta Konsthall, Schweden
2009 *Earth: Art of a changing world*, Royal Academy of Arts, UK
Rethink Kakotopia, Nikolaj Contemporary Art
Center, Kopenhagen, Dänemark
Life Forms, Bonniers Konsthall, Schweden
Wanås goes Green, Wanås Foundation, Schweden
Pastiche, Sølyst, Jyderup, Dänemark
Radical Nature, Barbican Art Gallery, London, UK
This World and Nearer Ones, Creative Time,
New York, USA
Seaux Garden Project, South London Gallery,
London, UK
Deep Green, Den Frie, Kopenhagen, Dänemark
Green Platform, Fondazione Palazzo Strozzi,
Florenz, Italien
2008 *Ein Bessere Welt*, Bonner Kunstverein, Deutschland
Frieze Projects 2008, Frieze Art Fair 2008, London, UK
Moralische Fantasien, Kunstmuseum Thurgau,
Kartause Ittingen, Schweiz
Supernatural, Kunsthalle Andratx, Mallorca, Spanien
Rauma Biennial 2008, Rauma, Finnland
Greenwashing, Fondazione Sandretto Re
Rebaudengo Turin, Italien
Salon 94, New York, USA
Karriere Bar, Kopenhagen, Dänemark
2007 *Von Ort zu Ort. Lichtkunstwerke in Parks, Villen und
Museen*, Winterthur, Schweiz
Kunstmaschinen Maschinenkunst, Schirn Kunsthalle, Frankfurt am Main
Skulptur Projekte 07, Münster
Made in Germany, Sprengel Museum, Hannover
Still Life: Art, Ecology and the politics of change,
Sharjah Biennial, UAE
Modelle für Morgen, European Kunsthalle, Köln
le mythe du cargo, Gallery Fernand Leger, Ivry,
Paris, Frankreich
2006 *Momentum*, Nordic Festival of contemporary art,
Norwegen

Inaugural Exhibition, Johann König, Berlin
Apocalypse Focus Group, ALP galleri Peter Bergman, Stockholm, Schweden
4, Anna Helwing Gallery, Los Angeles, USA
CLUSTER, PARTICIPANT INC., New York, USA
Jagdsalon, Kunstraum Kreuzberg, Berlin

2005 *Lichtkunst aus Kunstlicht*, ZKM, Karlsruhe
Threshold, Max Wigram Gallery, London, UK
Selected to post it, ICA, London, UK

2004 *L´attitude des autres*, SMP, Marseille, Frankreich
Tuesday is gone, Tblisi, Georgien
Black Friday. Exercises in Hermetics, Galerie Kamm, Berlin
Suburbia, Reggio Emilia, Italien
Ce qui reste, Galerie du TNB, Rennes, Frankreich
Prisma, Galerie Martin Janda, Wien, Österreich

2003 Gallery Beaumontpublic + königsbloc, Luxembourg
Absolvenz, Abschlussausstellung der Städelschule 2003, Frankfurt am Main
The state of the upper floor: Panorama / Total Motiviert, Kunstverein München
one place after another, Luftraum, Frankfurt am Main Airport, Frankfurt am Main
Bayrle, Greenfort, Zybach, Galerie Francesca Pia, Bern, Schweiz
The sky beneath your window, Zero, Paolo Zani, Piacenza, Italien
Posthorngasse 6/21 (Pernille K. Williams/Tue Greenfort), Wien, Österreich
Artforum Berlin, Johann König, Berlin
Rundgang, Städelschule, Frankfurt am Main

2001 *Jahresgabe 01/02*, Frankfurter Kunstverein, Frankfurt am Main
Vasistas, Teknik Üniversitesi, Istanbul, Turkei
Real Presence, Generation 2000, Museum 25. Maj, Belgrad, Serbien
Rundgang, Städelschule, Frankfurt am Main

Bibliografie (Auswahl) / Bibliography (Selection)

2012 Artforum, April 2012, T.J. Demos, *Art After Nature*, S. 194

2011 *Based in Berlin*, S. 84–85
Monopol, Interview mit Wolfram Putz, Friedrich von Borries, Tue Greenfort, Heft 3/2011, S. 50–55
Secession Katalog, Wien
APOGEE, A Compilation of Solitude, Ecology and Recreation
Buchprojekt von NÜANS

2010 RESIDUAL, Ausstellungskatalog Goethe Institut
The Institute of Lost Research, SITE Heft 12
the woods that see and hear, Ausstellungskatalog von Dertien Hectare
Powergames, Ludwig Muzeum, S. 30–33

2009 Elna Svenle, *Wanås 2009: Footprints,* Tue Greenfort, S. 12–15
This World & Nearer Ones, NYC, S. 50–51
Green Platform, Art Ecology Sustainability, Palazzo Strozzi, S. 96–97
Works of art in the heart of nature, S. 71–83
Radical Nature, Barbican Art Gallery, S. 135–142

2008 *Life Forms*, Albert Bonniers Förlag, *Incineration*, S. 44–50
‚Kunst und Klima/Art and Climate, Moralische Fantasien /Moral Imagination,
Verlag für Moderne Kunst Nürnberg, S. 92–95
André Rottmann, *Park Life, Über Tue Greenfort im Kunstverein Brauschweig,*
Texte zur Kunst, Berlin, 2008 S. 226–230
Susan Grønbech, ‚Kunstneren som nægter at være superstjerne* Børsen Kultur,
23. Juli 2008, S. 33

2007 *Nachvollziehungsangebote*, Kunsthalle Exnergasse, 1 Liter weniger – J.Grander
Ausstellungskatalog Sculpture Projects Münster 07, S. 116–121
Monopol Magazin für Kunst und Leben, S. 52–57
Dominic Eichler, *Making Do*, Frieze Mai–June Edition 2007, S. 208–213
Tema Celeste Contemorary Art Heft 121, S. 60–65

2006 Land, Art: a cultural ecology handbook, S. 116–125
RSA Journal, S. 24–29
TimeOut London, Dezember 6–13, 2006
Light Art from Artificial Light, Ausstellungskatalog ZKM, S. 618–619
Overblik – 63 danske samtidskunstnere, S. 232–235
Raimar Stange, SPIKE, 09 Herbst 2006, S. 56–63
Frieze, November–December 2006, Heft 103, S. 159–160
Ausstellungskatalog Momentum 2006, S. 64–67
Mark Sladen, *First Take*, Artforum, January 2006, S. 196–197
Max Andrews, *Tue Greenfort*, Wonderland Heft 2, Dec 05–Jan 06, S. 178–183

2005 Max Andrews, *Tue Greenfort*, W-Art, Heft 7, November 2005, S. 16–25
Catrin Loch, *Tue Greenfort*, Frieze, Heft 95
Raimar Stange, *Die Kunst der Ökologischen Praxis*, Kunst-Bulletin, Mai/Juni

2004 Knut Ebeling, *Ce qui reste*, FRAG Bretagne & Revolver, S. 23–25
Marco Senaldi, *Suburbia*, Reggio Emilia, S. 102
Daniel Bauman, *Kunst-Bulletin*, Jan/Feb 04, S. 42

2003 *Jahresring 50*, page 180, Oktagon, Cologne
Elmgren & Dragset: Spaced Out, Portikus, Frankfurt / M. S. 24–25
ArtReview, Volume LIV, July, S. 55

2002 *Gasthof 2002 Städelschule*, Frankfurt am Main
Clemens Krümmel, *Kuckuck*, Texte zur Kunste, Heft 48, December 2002
Janneke de Vries, *Bild-Portrait Tue Greenfort*, Artkaleidoscope Heft 2/02

Autoren
Contributors

Peder Anker

Peder Anker ist Privatdozent an der Gallatin School of Individualized Study sowie im Environmental Studies Program der New York University. Er veröffentlichte unter anderem: *Imperial Ecology: Environmental Order in the British Empire, 1895–1945*, Harvard University Press 2001, und *From Bauhaus to Eco-House: A History of Ecological Design*, Louisiana State University Press 2010.
www.pederanker.com

Peder Anker received his PhD in history of science from Harvard University in 1999. He is associate professor at the Gallatin School of Individualized Study and the Environmental Studies Program at New York University. His works include *Imperial Ecology: Environmental Order in the British Empire, 1895–1945* (Harvard University Press 2001) and *From Bauhaus to Eco-House: A History of Ecological Design* (Louisiana State University Press 2010).
www.pederanker.com

Severin Dünser

Severin Dünser arbeitet als Kurator im 21er Haus in Wien, wo er 2009 bis 2012 gemeinsam mit Christian Kobald den Ausstellungsraum COCO betrieb. Von 2002 bis 2005 leitete er Krinzinger Projekte. Daneben realisierte er zahlreiche Ausstellungen im In- und Ausland, u. a.: *Salon de la Kakanie*, Central House of Artists, Moskau, 2007; *Right Here, Right Now*, Fotohof Salzburg, 2009/2010; *Solace* (gem. mit C. Kobald, E. Layr und R. Vitorelli), Austrian Cultural Forum, New York, 2010; *Laokoon, Laokoon II*, COCO, Wien, 2010/2011; Franz Amann / Misha Stroj, Forum Stadtpark, Graz, 2011; *... sein Dasein verlässt und seine Gestalt der Erinnerung übergibt.* (gem. mit C. Kobald), curated_by Vienna 2011, Galerie Emanuel Layr; *Haltung und Ausdruck*, COCO, Wien, 2012.

Severin Dünser works as a curator at the 21er Haus in Vienna where, together with Christian Kobald, he has managed the exhibition room COCO. From 2002 to 2005 he headed the Krinzinger Projects. In addition he mounted many exhibitions nationally and internationally, among others: *Salon de la Kakanie*, Central House of Artists, Moscow, 2007; *Right Here, Right Now*, Fotohof Salzburg, 2009/2010; *Solace* (together with C. Kobald, E. Layr and R. Vitorelli), Austrian Cultural Forum, New York, 2010; *Laokoon, Laokoon II*, COCO, Vienna, 2010/2011; Franz Amann / Misha Stroj, Forum Stadtpark, Graz, 2011; *... sein Dasein verlässt und seine Gestalt der Erinnerung übergibt.* (together with C. Kobald), curated by Vienna 2011, Galerie Emanuel Layr; *Haltung und Ausdruck*, COCO, Vienna, 2012.

Dokumentation zur Ausstellung
Documentation of the exhibition

Tue Greenfort
Eine Berggeschichte
14. September – 4. November 2012

Ausstellung / Exhibition:
Montagehalle, Jahngasse 9
Büro / Office:
Marktstraße 33, A-6850 Dornbirn
Tel 0043-(0)5572-55044
Fax 0043-(0)5572-55044 4838
kunstraum@dornbirn.at
www.kunstraumdornbirn.at

Ausstellung / Exhibition
Kuratorin der Ausstellung / Curator of
the Exhibition:
Severin Dünser, Wien / Vienna
Organisation, Produktion / Organisation,
Production: Hans Dünser
Videodokumentation / Video Documentation:
Hans Jörg Kapeller

Kunstraum Dornbirn
Präsident / President: Ekkehard Bechtold
Leitung / Direction: Hans Dünser
PR / Marketing: Herta Pümpel
Sekretariat / Secretariat: Karin Dünser

Katalog / Catalog
Herausgeber / Editor:
Kunstraum Dornbirn, Hans Dünser
Gestaltung / Grafic Design:
Flax, Jutz, Mätzler Agentur für Kommunikation
Redaktion / Editing:
Herta Pümpel
Lektorat / Proofreading:
Verlag für moderne Kunst Nürnberg
Texte / Texts:
Severin Dünser, Peder Anker
Übersetzung / Translation:
Jeanne Haunschild, Bonn;
Stefan Barmann, Wien / Vienna

Fotonachweis / Photo credits
© Fessler Fotografie, Robert Fessler,
6923 Lauterach, Österreich / Austria

Schrift / Typeface:
News Gothic Regular / Italic / Bold
Papier / Paper:
Gemini weiß 300 g/qm,
Gmund Colors 300 g/qm, Clarobulk 150 g/qm
Druck / Print:
Buchdruckerei Lustenau GmbH, Millenium Park 10,
6890 Lustenau, Österreich / Austria

© Nürnberg 2012, Tue Greenfort, Verlag für
moderne Kunst Nürnberg und die Autoren /
and the authors

Alle Rechte vorbehalten / All Rights reserved

Printed in Austria
ISBN 978-3-86984-364-3

Bibliografische Information
Der Deutschen Nationalbibliothek
Die Deutsche Nationalbibliothek verzeichnet diese
Publikation in der Deutschen Nationalbibliografie;
detaillierte bibliografische Daten sind im Internet
über http://dnb.ddb.de abrufbar.

Bibliographic Information published by
Die Deutsche Nationalbibliothek
Die Deutsche Nationalbibliothek lists this
publication in the Deutschen Nationalbibliografie;
detailed bibliographic data is available in the
Internet at http://dnb.ddb.de

Distributed outside Europe
D.A.P. / Distributed Art Publishers, Inc.
155 Sixth Avenue, 2nd Floor, New York, NY 100
phone 001-(0)212-627 19 99,
fax 001-(0)212-627 94 84

Distributed in the United Kingdom
Cornerhouse Publications; 70 Oxford Street,
Manchester M 1 5 NH, UK
phone 0044-(0)161-200 15 03,
fax 0044-(0)161-200 15 04

Dank an die Autoren / Our thanks to the authors:
Severin Dünser, Wien / Vienna
Peder Anker, Oslo

Mit freundlicher Unterstützung / Thanks to:
Der Subventionsgeber:
Stadt Dornbirn, Land Vorarlberg und Republik
Österreich – bm:ukk, Kunstsektion.

Des Hauptsponsors des Kunstraum Dornbirn,
der Dornbirner Sparkasse Bank AG.

Ausstellungskataloge des Kunstraum Dornbirn
Exhibition Catalogs of the Kunstraum Dornbirn

www.kunstraumdornbirn.at

Lois und Franziska Weinberger
Wir sind des Baumes müde
32 S./pp.
Deutsch/English
ISBN 978-3-936711-26-4

Gloria Friedmann
Play-Back aus Eden
36 S./pp.
Deutsch/English
ISBN 978-3-936711-83-7

Teres Wydler
*N.I.C.E –
Nature in Corrosive Ecstasy©*
60 S./pp.
Deutsch/English
ISBN 978-3-939738-68-8

Tamara Grcic
lichtgrün, grün, feuille-morte
32 S./pp.
Deutsch/English
ISBN 978-3-936711-38-7

*Zerstörte Welten
und die Utopie der
Rekonstruktion*
108 S./pp.
Deutsch/English
ISBN 978-3-938821-74-9

Urs-P. Twellmann
Forstrevier 3
32 S./pp.
Deutsch/English
ISBN 978-3-939738-67-1

Tony Matelli
Fuck'd and The Oracle
40 S./pp.
Deutsch/English
ISBN 978-3-936711-57-8

Simon Wachsmuth
*die Dinge kann ich
nicht mehr sehn,
wie ich sie einmal sah*
32 S./pp.
Deutsch/English
ISBN 978-3-939738-13-8

Mark Dion
Concerning Hunting
160 S./pp.
English/Deutsch
ISBN 978-3775721974

Franz Huemer
*... der letze Rest vom
abgespaltenen Paradies*
36 S./pp.
Deutsch/English
ISBN 978-3-936711-76-9

Olaf Nicolai
Constantin
Künstlerbuch
28 S./pp.
Deutsch/English/Français
ISBN 978-3940064813

Simon Starling
Plant Room
32 S./pp.
Deutsch/English
ISBN 978-3-940748-75-1

Marco Evaristti
Pink State
40 S./pp.
Deutsch/English
ISBN 978-3-936711-82-0

Michel Blazy
Falling Garden
32 S./pp.
Deutsch/English
ISBN 978-3-939738-50-3

Roman Signer
Installation
Unfall als Skulptur
40 S./pp.
Deutsch/English
ISBN 978-3-940748-74-4

 **Igor Sacharow-Ross**
Nicht gefiltert
60 S./pp.
Deutsch/English
ISBN 978-3-941185-83-8

 **Peter Buggenhout**
caterpillar logic
60 S./pp.
Deutsch/English
ISBN 978-3-86984-133-5

 **Nin Brudermann**
Twelve O'Clock In London. Austria/Autriche
60 S./pp.
Deutsch/English
ISBN 978-3-86984-363-6

 **Fides Becker**
Ein Panorama
60 S./pp.
Deutsch/English
ISBN 978-3-941185-70-8

 **Alfred Graf**
Uni ver sal mus eum
60 S./pp.
Deutsch/English
ISBN 978-3-86984-243-1

 **Tue Greenfort**
Eine Berggeschichte
68 S./pp.
Deutsch/English
ISBN 978-3-86984-364-3

 **Mathias Kessler**
The Taste of Discovery
60 S./pp.
Deutsch/English
ISBN 978-3-941185-71-5

 **Erwin Wurm**
Narrow House
60 S./pp.
Deutsch/English
ISBN 978-3-86984-245-5

 **Jan Kopp**
Das endlose Spiel – Le jeu sans fin
60 S./pp.
Deutsch/English/Français
ISBN 978-3-86984-030-7

 **Didier Marcel**
Red Harvest
64 S./pp.
Deutsch/English/Français
ISBN 978-3-86984-247-9

 **Klaus Mosettig**
Nature morte
144 S./pp.
Deutsch/English
ISBN 978-3-86984-028-4

 **Not Vital**
Lasst hundert Blumen blühen
48 S./pp.
Deutsch/English
ISBN 978-3-86984-348-3